Volume

15 ml	$^1/_2$ fl oz
30 ml	1 fl oz
50 ml	2 fl oz
75 ml	$2^1/_2$ fl oz
100 ml	$3^1/_2$ fl oz
125 ml	4 fl oz
150 ml	5 fl oz ($^1/_4$ pint)
175 ml	6 fl oz
200 ml	7 fl oz

225 ml	8 fl oz
250 ml	9 fl oz
300 ml	10 fl oz ($^1/_2$ pint)
600 ml	20 fl oz (1 pint)
750 ml	$1^1/_4$ pints
1 litre	$1^3/_4$ pints
2 litre	$3^1/_2$ pints
2.2 litres	4 pints
3 litres	$5^1/_2$ pints

Spoons

1.25 ml	$^1/_4$ teaspoon
2.5 ml	$^1/_2$ teaspoon
5 ml	1 teaspoon
10 ml	2 teaspoons
15 ml	1 tablespoon
30 ml	2 tablespoons
45 ml	3 tablespoons
60 ml	4 tablespoons
75 ml	5 tablespoons
90 ml	6 tablespoons
105 ml	7 tablespoons
120 ml	8 tablespoons

Linear

5 mm	$^1/_4$ inch
1 cm	$^1/_2$ inch
2.5 cm	1 inch
5 cm	2 inches
7.5 cm	3 inches
9 cm	$3^1/_2$ inches
10 cm	4 inches
13 cm	5 inches
15 cm	6 inches
18 cm	7 inches
20 cm	8 inches
23 cm	9 inches
25.5 cm	10 inches
28 cm	11 inches
30 cm	12 inches (1 foot)

Seasonal Country Kitchen

Seasonal Country Kitchen

NIKKI ROWAN-KEDGE
AND
ANGELA RAWSON

° THE °
SPORTSMAN'S
PRESS

Acknowledgement

The poem on page 91, 'Upper Lambourne', by John Betjeman is from *Collected Poems* and is reproduced by permission of John Murray (Publishers) Ltd.

Copyright © 2007 Nikki Rowan-Kedge & Angela Rawson
Illustrations by Angela Rawson

First published in the UK in 2007
by The Sportsman's Press, an imprint of Quiller Publishing Ltd

British Library Cataloguing-in-Publication Data
A catalogue record for this book
is available from the British Library

ISBN 978 1 904057 95 6

Printed in China

The Sportsman's Press

An imprint of Quiller Publishing Ltd
Wykey House, Wykey, Shrewsbury, SY4 1JA
Tel: 01939 261616 Fax: 01939 261606
E-mail: info@quillerbooks.com
Website: www.countrybooksdirect.com

CONTENTS

Spring

Soups

Starters and Side-Dishes

Fish

Main Courses

Puddings

Cakes

Summer

Soups

Starters and Side-Dishes

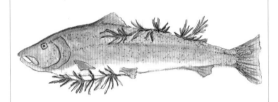

Autumn

Soups

Carrot and Coriander Soup 118

Chestnut and Smoked Bacon Soup 119

Curried Pumpkin Soup 120

Hunter's Soup 121

Roasted Garlic and Marrow Soup 122

Tomato and Orange Soup 123

Starters and Side-Dishes

Bacon and Herb Patties 124

Clotted Cream and Caviar Savoury 126

Double Cooked Roquefort Soufflé 127

Mushrooms with Garlic and Chicken Liver
  Pâté 129

Potted Pheasant with Crab Apple Jelly 131

Fish

Cod Roasted with a Cheese and Herb
  Crust 132

Devilled Crab 133

Kipper Cakes 135

Fillets of Plaice with Lime and Basil
  Butter Sauce 136

Stuffed River Trout with Almond
  Sauce 138

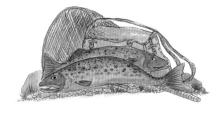

Main Courses

Chicken and Herb Patties 140

Drambuie Duck with Orange Sauce 141

Lamb Fillet in Puff Pastry with
  Shrewsbury Sauce 143

Pork Cutlets with Apple Mayonnaise 145

Farmhouse Rabbit Stew with Raisins 146

Game Pie 147

Hedgerow Pheasant Casserole 149

Sautéed Pheasant Breasts with Chestnut
  Sauce 151

Venison and Beer Hot-Pot 152

Wild Duck with Apricots 153

Puddings

Cakes

Drinks

Preserves

Winter

Soups

Starters and Side-Dishes

Fish

Anchovy Toast 180

Baked Pike with Onion and
  Herb Sauce 181

Fish Quenelles with Orange Sauce 183

Scottish Kipper Pâté with Whisky and
  Lime 185

Smoked Haddock with Poached Egg 186

Puddings

Brandied Orange-Filled Prunes 204

Dark Chocolate Pudding with Whisky and
  Honey Sauce 205

Hot Coffee Fudge Pudding 207

Hot Rum Bananas 208

Iced Cointreau and Raisin Mousse 209

Pink Champagne, Pomegranate and Pink
  Grapefruit Sorbet 210

Plum, Date and Cinnamon Crumble 212

Rum and Raisin Semi-Freddo 213

Main Courses

Carbonade of Vegetables with Cheese
  Scone Topping 188

Spicy Duck Sausages 190

Turkey Fillets with Lime and Green
  Grape Sauce 191

Goose Roasted with Prune, Quince
  and Apple 192

Hashed Pheasant 194

Pork and Bean Hot-Pot 195

Pot-Port Braised Pheasant 196

Roast Partridge in a Pear Sauce 197

Roast Woodcock 199

Saddle of Hare with Blackberry Sauce 200

Venison and Beefsteak Suet Crust
  Pudding 202

Cakes

Courgette and Sultana Muffins 214

Dark Treacle Gingerbread Cake 216

Gamekeeper's Fruit Cake 217

Maple Butter Cake 219

Pocket Ginger Flapjacks 220

Stock, Sauce and Marinade

Smoked Ham Sauce 221

Spicy Tomato Sauce 222

Quick Game Bird Stock 223

Marinade for Venison 224

Spring

SOUPS

Cream of Asparagus and Coconut Soup

Mr Jorrocks sat in expectation . . . as the first spoonful passed before his eyes. 'My vig, why it's water!' exclaimed he – 'water I do declare, with worms in it – I can't eat such stuff as that – it's not man's meat–oh! dear, oh! dear, I fear I've made a terrible mistake in coming to France!'

(Jorrocks' Jaunts and Jollities, R. S. Surtees)

Poor old Jorrocks, how he must have longed for a plate of English style soup such as this cream of asparagus, even with the addition of 'foreign' creamed coconut which gives the soup its smooth, creamy texture and delicate flavour.

Ingredients to serve 4

3 tablespoons olive oil

2 medium onions, peeled and chopped

450 g (1 lb) asparagus, cleaned, trimmed and
   evenly chopped

750 ml (1$\frac{1}{4}$ pints) vegetable or chicken stock

150 g (5 $\frac{1}{2}$ oz) piece creamed coconut

Sea salt and freshly ground black pepper
   to taste

Method

Heat the oil in a saucepan. Put in the onion and cook until just beginning to soften. Pour in the stock, add the asparagus, stir in the creamed coconut and season to taste. Bring to simmering point and cook for 15 minutes. Remove from the heat and drain off the liquid into a bowl. Put the onion and asparagus into a food processor and whiz until smooth. Transfer the purée to the soup liquid and return to a saucepan. Check the seasonings and re-heat when ready to eat.

Celeriac and Almond Soup

Celeriac, as its name implies, has the strong flavour of celery. Buy the smoothest celeriac you can, it makes peeling much easier and there is less waste.

Ingredients to serve 4–6

4 tablespoons olive oil

1 large onion, peeled and finely chopped

1 celeriac, peeled and chopped into pieces

1 clove garlic, crushed

850 ml (1$^1/_2$ pints) chicken or vegetable stock

Sea salt and freshly ground black pepper to taste

100 ml (3$^1/_2$ fl oz) double cream

2 tablespoons slivered almonds, lightly toasted

Method

Heat the oil in a saucepan add the onion, cook until soft and then add the chopped celeriac and crushed garlic. Cook for a couple of minutes, pour in the stock, season to taste and cook for 15–20 minutes. (The time will depend upon the size of the celeriac pieces, the smaller they are, the quicker they will cook.)

Once the celeriac is soft remove from the heat and allow to cool a little before liquidising until smooth. Return the soup to a clean saucepan, re-heat gently, stirring in the cream. Check seasonings and pour the soup into warm soup bowls, scatter over toasted slivered almonds.

Cook's note
If the soup is too thick for your liking, slacken with a little milk or water

Mulligatawny

'When the heavy lazy mist, which hangs over every object, making the gas lamps look brighter, and dining parlour curtains are closely drawn, kitchen fires blaze brightly up, and savoury steams of hot dinners salute the nostrils of the hungry wayfarer.'

(*Sketches by Boz,* Charles Dickens)

It is generally believed that British officers and diplomats serving in India brought this spicy soup to British shores. Nourishing and tasty, it is ideal for flasks when out in rough weather or as a warm welcome home after a day in the open air.

Ingredients to serve 4–6

1 tablespoon beef dripping

2 large onions, peeled and chopped

2 carrots, peeled and chopped

3 sticks celery, washed and chopped

1 clove garlic, crushed

1 tablespoon plain flour

1 litre (1³/₄ pints) meat stock

1 tablespoon mango chutney, large lumps chopped

4 teaspoons curry paste

70 g (2¹/₂ oz) diced cooked lamb or beef

1 tablespoon chopped parsley

2 teaspoons tomato paste

Sea salt and ground black pepper

Method

Melt the dripping in a large pan. Add the chopped onion, carrot, celery and crushed garlic. Cook until the vegetables are just turning brown. Add the flour to the pan and stir thoroughly for a few minutes to cook the flour. Pour in the meat stock and simmer for 30–40 minutes until the vegetables are cooked. Mix in the chutney, curry paste, diced meat, chopped parsley and tomato paste; season well to taste. Stir and cook for a further 15 minutes. Serve with warm crusty bread and a glass of tawny port.

Cook's note
A good meat stock is necessary for a well-flavoured Mulligatawny.

Mushroom and Green Peppercorn Soup

'A wild night and a lonely one, a night for a man to saddle his horse and gallop into the teeth of the wind on a high heath with his eyes to the far sea and his cheeks whipped with racing blood.'

(*Wild Wings and Some Footsteps,* J. Wentworth Day)

Ingredients to serve 4

3 tablespoons olive oil

1 medium sized onion, peeled and finely chopped

1 clove garlic, crushed

225 g (8 oz) button or chestnut mushrooms, wiped and sliced

1 litre (1³/₄ pints) vegetable stock

1 rounded teaspoon green peppercorns

100 ml (3.5 fl oz) double or single cream

Sea salt to taste

Method

Heat the oil in a saucepan. Put in the onion and cook until soft, then add the crushed garlic, mushroom slices and cook for 1 minute. Pour in the stock, add the peppercorns and sea salt to taste. Simmer for 10 minutes. If you have a hand liquidiser, whiz in the pan until smooth, stir in the cream.

For food processors Allow the soup to cool a little and liquidise until smooth. Return to the pan, stir in the cream. Re-heat to serve.

Tomato and Roasted Red Pepper Soup

'They took my sleeve to strain the soup' repeated Philippa, in a crystal clarity of wrath. 'She said she got it in the press in the passage ma'am, and she thought you were after throwin' it' murmured Hannah, with a glance that implored my support.

(*Further Experiences of an Irish R. M,* E. OE, Somerville and Martin Ross)

Roasting the peppers can be done well in advance; they should keep in the refrigerator for up to 4–5 days in an airtight container. The soup does not need to be strained, so your dress sleeves are quite safe.

Ingredients to serve 4–6

4 tablespoons olive oil

2 medium onions, peeled and chopped

2 roasted red peppers, skin removed

900 g (2 lb) tomatoes, skinned and chopped

1 clove garlic, crushed

600 ml (1 pint) chicken stock

300 ml (¹/₂ pint) tomato juice

2 tablespoons honey

4 teaspoons tomato paste

2 teaspoons sundried tomato paste

Sea salt and ground black pepper to taste

1 bay leaf

2 tablespoons freshly chopped basil leaves

Method

To roast the peppers

Pre-heat the oven to 200ºC/400ºF/gas mark 6. Cut the peppers in half, remove the stalk, core and seeds. Lay them cut side down on a baking tray; brush over olive oil and put into the oven to roast for approximately 15 minutes until the skin begins to 'blister'. Remove from the oven and peel away the skin.

To make the soup Heat the oil in a large saucepan and add all the ingredients except the chopped basil. Simmer for 20 minutes; remove the bay leaf and discard. Allow the soup to cool slightly, then liquidise. Stir in the basil, reheat when required.

Stilton and Spring Onion Soup

Sweet are the sounds that mingle from afar,
Heard by the calm lakes, as peeps the folding star,
Where the duck dabbles mid the rustling sedge,
And feeding pike starts from the water's edge.

(*An Evening Walk*, William Wordsworth)

This is a very creamy, delicious soup, easy to make and transport. Ideal for lunch by the river bank.

Ingredients to serve 4–6

3 tablespoons olive oil

1 medium onion, peeled and chopped

2 sticks celery, washed and chopped

2 carrots, peeled and chopped

8 spring onions peeled and chopped

1 clove garlic crushed with a little salt

$^3/_4$ litre ($1^1/_4$ pints) chicken or vegetable stock

Sea salt and ground black pepper

125 g ($4^1/_2$ oz) Stilton cheese, rind removed

125 ml (4 fl oz) single cream

Method

Melt the oil in a large, heavy-based pan, add the chopped vegetables and crushed garlic. Cook until the vegetables are soft, stirring occasionally. When the vegetables are cooked, pour in the stock and season well. Simmer for $^1/_2$ hour, then remove from the heat and crumble the cheese into the liquid. Mix well, then purée the soup in a blender; pour into a clean saucepan, stir in the cream and re-heat when required.

Cook's note

If serving this soup at home, 2 of the spring onions can be reserved then chopped and added raw or sautéed in a little butter and scattered over the soup before serving.

STARTERS AND SIDE-DISHES

Celeriac and Egg Salad

Good for a light snack or as a side-salad to accompany a main course. The eggs must not be boiled for longer than 5–6 minutes. Plunge into cold water to prevent further cooking, this eliminates those dark circles around the egg yolks, which not only look unsightly, but also mean the eggs will be over cooked and rubbery.

Ingredients to serve

400 g (14 oz) shredded celeriac

2 tablespoons light mayonnaise

1 tablespoon chopped chives

2 eggs, hard-boiled

4 tablespoons vinaigrette dressing

Method

Put the shredded celeriac into a mixing bowl and pour over the dressing. Toss and allow to stand for 30 minutes. Shell the hard-boiled eggs and chop the whites. Mix with the celeriac and blend in the mayonnaise. Sieve the egg yolks over the top of the salad and sprinkle with chopped chives.

Cook's note
Sieving the egg yolk is optional – the yolks can of course just be cut into pieces.

Green Peppercorn and Pea Timbale

Ingredients to serve 2–4

500 g (1 lb 2 oz) fresh or frozen peas

2 teaspoons green peppercorns

4 tablespoons soft breadcrumbs

2 tablespoons milk

Salt and black pepper to taste

70 g (2$^1/_2$ oz) softened butter

3 free-range eggs, separated

A little grated parmesan cheese to serve

Method

Cook the peas in a little water for 5 minutes, drain and put into a food processor; add the peppercorns and liquidise to a smooth purée. Soak the breadcrumbs in the milk. Turn the purée into a mixing bowl. Over a basin, drain the soaked breadcrumbs through a sieve, pressing down with the back of a spoon. Stir the drained breadcrumbs into the pea purée. Season to taste and then blend in the softened butter. Beat the egg yolks and stir into the purée. Whip the egg whites until stiff and fold into the pea purée.

Put the purée into a buttered basin and place in a steamer. Cover, bring to the boil and steam for 1 hour.

Turn the timbale out onto a warm serving plate, sprinkle over a little grated Parmesan cheese and serve.

Cook's note
The mixture can be put into individual timbales instead of a basin if preferred and steamed in the same way. They will take approximately 20–25 minutes depending on the size of timbales.

Pea Purée with Quail Eggs and Bacon

The host must provide for the pleasure of the company, the guest must try to make his company pleasant.

The Pleasure of Your Company, June and Doris Langley Moore.

Some good advice, especially first thing in the morning. This dish is great for breakfast, a little different from the normal eggs and bacon.

Ingredients to serve 2

250 g (9 oz) fresh or frozen peas

40 g (1½ oz) butter

3 tablespoons double cream

Salt and white pepper

6 quail eggs

6 rashers smoked, streaky bacon, rind removed

Method

Cook the peas in a little boiling water until tender. Drain and put into a food processor; add the butter, double cream and season to taste. Liquidise until smooth, turn out into a bowl and keep warm.

Boil the eggs for 3–4 minutes, and then remove from the water. Allow to cool a little before removing the shell keeping the eggs whole.

Fry the bacon until crispy, then cut it into pieces. Divide the purée between two warm plates, top with the boiled quail eggs and sprinkle over crispy bacon pieces. Serve with hot toast or hot crusty bread.

Cook's note
To save time, bacon already chopped into pieces can be bought from most good supermarkets.

Peppered Cheese Tartlets

The piece of flummery being delivered, the bottles and dessert circulated and in due time, the ladies retired, the Misses to the drawing room, Madam to the pantry, to see that the Bumbler had not pocketed any of the cheesecakes or tarts, for which, boy-like, he had a propensity…

(*Ask Mama*, R. S. Surtees)

Ingredients to make 20–24 small tartlets

For the pastry
100 g (3½ oz) butter
100 g (3½ oz) finely grated Cheddar cheese
Pinch of sea salt
¼ teaspoon cayenne pepper
125 g (4½ oz) plain flour

For the filling
250 g (9 oz) cottage cheese
125 ml (4 fl oz) single cream
100 g (3½ oz) grated strong Cheddar or other
  good flavoured hard cheese
2 eggs
Cayenne pepper and black pepper to taste
Sea salt to taste

Method

To make the pastry Put the butter and grated cheese into a food processor, blend together until smooth; add the flour and the seasonings; whiz until the pastry forms a dough. Turn out of the processor and wrap in a polythene bag and leave it to rest for 30 minutes in a fridge.

To make the filling Put the clotted cheese and cream into the food processor, cream together until smooth, add the grated cheese, eggs and seasonings. Blend again until creamy.

Pre-heat the oven to 200ºC/400ºF/gas mark 6 Roll out the pastry and cut into circles and line the tartlet tins with pastry rings. Spoon in the filling and cook for approximately 10–12 minutes until golden brown. Serve hot from the oven.

Warm Spinach, Asparagus and Goat's Cheese Salad

Ingredients to serve 6–8 as a starter or 4 as a main course

500 g (1 lb 2 oz) spinach, washed, tough stalks removed

1 tablespoon olive oil

Salt and ground black pepper

16 spears fresh asparagus

70 g (2$\frac{1}{2}$ oz) grated or very thinly sliced goat's cheddar cheese

Method

Cook the spinach in a steamer or in a very small amount of boiling water until just soft: it needs to be cooked but still retain its crispness. Drain thoroughly. Drizzle over the olive oil, season to taste, mix well together, breaking up any large leaves.

Steam the asparagus for a few minutes. Divide the spinach evenly between warm plates and place the asparagus spears on top of each pile of spinach. Season once more and sprinkle over the grated or sliced goat's cheese.

Cook's note

The spinach can be laid upon slices of hot garlic bread for a more substantial meal, or served separate as an accompaniment.

FISH

Crab Mousse with Avocado Sauce

'Buy my flounders twelve pence a peck' 'Crab, crab, any crab'
'Hot baked wardens, all fresh and fair'

(Peddlers' and Market Cries, London)

Ingredients to serve 6–8

1 tin crab soup

2 tablespoons mayonnaise

350 g (12 oz) light cream cheese

Finely grated rind and juice of 2 small lemons

3 sheets leaf gelatine, soaked in a little water

300 ml (½ pint) whipping cream

450 g (1 lb) white and brown crab meat

Sea salt and black to taste

For the sauce

2 large ripe avocados, peeled, stone removed

Juice of 1 lemon

A little milk to slacken the sauce

Sea salt and black pepper to taste

Method

Put the soup, mayonnaise, cream cheese, lemon rind and juice into a food processor or liquidiser and blend until smooth. Season to taste. Drain the cold water from the gelatine then dissolve in 3½ tablespoons boiling water. When dissolved, put into the food processor, blend again and then transfer the mixture to a mixing bowl.

Whip the cream and fold into the mixture, then mix in the crab meat. Check the seasonings, pour into a dish, cover and refrigerate to set.

When ready to serve the mousse, if using individual moulds, run a knife around the edge of the moulds to loosen and turn out onto a plate. If using one large bowl spoon from the dish.

To make the sauce Put the avocado flesh and lemon juice into a liquidizer with a little milk. Blend until smooth, adding a little more milk as and when necessary. Season. Serve separately in a sauce boat or pour around the mousse.

Crunchy Trout Pie

Prepared in advance, this is an ideal dish for any traveller or sportsman coming home at the end of the day; just re-heat in the oven when required.

Ingredients to serve 4

450 g (1 lb) trout fillets, skin and any bones
  removed
300 ml ($^1/_2$ pint) milk
70 g ($2^1/_2$ oz) unsalted butter
1 medium onion, peeled and finely chopped
25 g (1 oz) plain flour
1 tin anchovy fillets, drained and chopped

2 teaspoons tomato paste
4 tablespoons double cream
1 tablespoon tarragon, chopped
Freshly ground black pepper
100 g ($3^1/_2$ oz) wholemeal breadcrumbs mixed
  with 3 tablespoons olive oil

Method

Pre-heat the oven to 190ºC/375ºF/gas mark 5. Pour the milk into a saucepan, put in the trout fillets and poach gently until lightly cooked. Strain the milk into a basin and reserve, flake the fish into chunks and set aside. Put half the amount of the butter into a saucepan, add the chopped onion and cook until soft. Remove the onion and put to one side, put the remaining butter into the pan, stir in the flour and cook for 2 minutes. Gradually pour in the poaching milk stirring all the time, blending to a smooth sauce. Mix the cooked onion, chopped anchovies, tomato paste, cream, chopped tarragon and black pepper to taste into the sauce mixture and then lightly fold in the flaked fish. Pile into an ovenproof dish; scatter the oil-soaked breadcrumbs evenly over the top and bake in the oven for 35 minutes until the top is golden brown and crunchy.

Cook's note
If the dish is not to be eaten immediately after preparing, it needs to be cooked for 45–50 minutes.

Devilled Pike

In the days when poaching was necessary to break a monotonous diet of bread, fat bacon and cheese, a fresh pike would have been most welcome. A still, sunny day was required, usually in early spring, too many ripples made it difficult to spot the fish. A long, thin ash or hazel stick with a wire noose at one end was the only tool required. Once the wire noose was past the fins, a quick jerk and the pike was on the bank…

Ingredients to serve 4

500 g (1 lb 2 oz) filleted pike

2 tablespoons plain flour sifted with a little
  salt and cayenne pepper

4 tablespoons olive oil

100 ml (3^1/$_2$ fl oz) tarragon vinegar

2 tablespoons clear honey

1 clove garlic, crushed

4 shallots, peeled and chopped

1 level teaspoon ground mace

1 level teaspoon curry paste

Sea salt and black pepper

Method

Cut the pike flesh into pieces and dust with the seasoned flour. Heat the oil in a frying pan and sauté until crisp and brown. Put all the other ingredients into a saucepan, add the browned fish, stir gently so as not to break up the fish chunks, cover, and simmer for 15 minutes.

Serving suggestion Brown rice and a green salad.

Cook's note
To fillet the pike. Cut off the head, slit along the belly and clean out well. Spread the fish apart cut side down, press along the backbone until you feel it 'give', turn the fish over and remove the backbone and as many bones as you can find. Scrape the flesh away from the skin.

Fisherman's Hot-Pot

> But yet while I freely fish, I fast,
> I make good fortune my repast;
> And thereunto my friend invite,
> In whom I more than that delight:
> Who is more welcome to my dish
> Than to my angle was my fish.
>
> (*The Angler's Song,* William Basse)

A good dish for using up any left-over hard cheese or cooked potatoes. New potatoes can be used unpeeled and sliced if preferred.

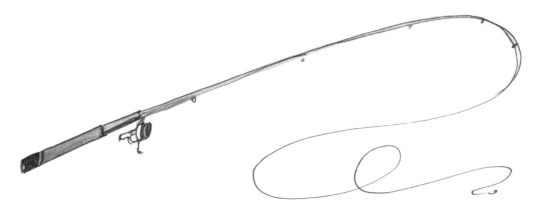

Ingredients to serve 4

500 g (1 lb 2 oz) cod fillet, skin removed and
  any bones

650 g (1½ lb) potatoes, peeled and boiled

Juice of 1 small lemon

2 tablespoons butter

1 medium onion, peeled and sliced

225 g (8 oz) chestnut mushrooms, cleaned
  and sliced

1 tablespoon cornflour, slackened with
3 tablespoons milk

150 ml (¼ pint) whole milk

125 g (4½ oz) grated Cheddar or other
  strong-flavoured cheese

Sea salt and black pepper to taste

Method

Line an ovenproof dish with a layer of thinly sliced boiled potato, reserving some potato for the top. Cut the fish into chunks and layer half the amount on top of the potato. Pour half the quantity of lemon juice over the fish. Melt the butter in a frying pan and fry the onion until just beginning to change colour and then tip over the fish. Lay all the mushroom slices over the onion, lay the remaining fish over the mushrooms.

Pour the slackened cornflour into a saucepan, add the milk, and half the amount of grated cheese. Heat gently stirring all the time until slightly thickened, do not boil. Pour the cheese and milk over the fish, cover with the remaining potato slices and sprinkle over the remaining grated cheese. Bake uncovered in the oven at 200ºC/400ºF/gas mark 6 for 40 minutes until the top is golden brown and the cheese is bubbling.

Hot Scallop and Haddock Terrine

No need to make your own fish stock as liquid fish stock can be bought from most good supermarkets in sealed packs or jars or you can use fish stock cubes.

Ingredients for approximately 4 servings

500 g (1 lb 2 oz) fresh haddock, skin and
  bones removed

6 fresh scallops, trimmed coral removed

2 free-range eggs

75 ml double cream

Sea salt and ground black pepper

For the panade

225 ml (7 fl oz) whole milk

2 chopped shallots

1 small carrot chopped into matchstick-sized
  pieces

1 small bay leaf

1 small stick celery, cut into small sticks

1 small piece mace

60 g (2$^1/_4$ oz) unsalted butter

75 g (3 oz) plain flour

For the sauce

12 large shelled prawns – heads discarded (tail
  and body shell reserved for the butter)

35 g (1$^1/_4$oz) unsalted butter

$^1/_2$ teaspoon paprika

1 tablespoon plain flour

Rind and juice of $^1/_2$ lemon

200 ml (7 fl oz) fish stock

$^1/_2$ sherry glass Amontillado sherry

3 tablespoons double cream

Method

To make the panade This can be done the day before. Pour the milk into a saucepan, add the chopped shallot, carrot, bay leaf, celery and mace. Bring to simmering point then remove from the heat. Allow to stand to infuse for 10 minutes. Strain and reserve the flavoured milk. Return the strained and flavoured milk to the saucepan, add the butter and bring to the boil. Remove from the heat and beat in the flour until smooth. Put to one side to cool.

To prepare the fish Cut the haddock into chunks and put into a food blender with the cooled panade. Blend until the lumps have disappeared. Do not over-mix, just enough to blend together. Add the eggs and cream; season to taste and blend again. Transfer the fish mixture into a bowl and stir in the chopped scallop coral. Fill an ovenproof dish with half the haddock mixture.

Slice the white scallop meat fairly thickly then lay the slices down the centre of the haddock mixture in the dish. Put in the remaining haddock mixture, spreading evenly. Cover with buttered greaseproof paper, and then lay a double piece of foil over the top to seal in the flavour.

To make the sauce Pound the prawn shells with the butter in a pestle and mortar to extract the flavour from the shells. Put into a small saucepan and heat until the butter has melted. Strain away the shells and discard. Return the flavoured butter to a clean saucepan, add the paprika and cook gently for 1 minute then add the flour and cook gently until 'marbled'. Remove from the heat and stir in the fish stock. Return to the heat, bring to the boil stirring all the time until the sauce has thickened and then add the lemon juice and rind and sherry, blending it all well in. Lower the heat right down and stir in the cream and shelled prawns. The sauce must not boil at this stage. Serve with the hot terrine.

Cook's note
Individual terrines may be used or a small loaf tin. If a cold terrine is required, it can be served without the sauce – allow the terrine to cool and put into the refrigerator. Remove at least $1/2$ hour before serving. If it's too cold it will not have much of a flavour.

For extra taste, flavour the butter used in the panade.

Kedgeree

Khichari, or Kedgeree, originally came from India and was brought to Britain in the nineteenth century by members of the East India Company. It consisted of spices, lentils, rice, limes, fish and butter and graced the sideboards the country house dining rooms for breakfast, alongside dishes of kidneys, bacon, eggs and ham. Though the first meal of the day is not the leisurely affair it used to be, it is nonetheless an excellent dish on which to start the day, especially as it can be made a day or so before. Kedgeree is a versatile dish, excellent for lunch or light supper and easily transportable for picnics.

By using flaked salmon instead of the usual smoked haddock, it makes a delicious first course for a spring dinner party.

Ingredients to serve 4–6

300 ml (¹/₂ pint) whole milk

500 g (1 lb 2 oz) salmon fillet, skin and stray
  bones removed

170 g (6 oz) long grain rice

115 g (4 oz) unsalted butter

2 medium onions, peeled and chopped

6 hard-boiled eggs, shelled and chopped

Grated rind and juice of 2 limes and 1 lemon

1 teaspoon cayenne pepper

1 teaspoon paprika

2 rounded tablespoons parsley, chopped

Sea salt to taste

125 ml (4 fl oz) double cream

Method

Pour the milk into a saucepan, put in the salmon fillet and poach until tender. Remove the fish, leaving the milk in the pan. Put the rice into the milk and cook until soft, adding a little water if necessary. While the rice is cooking, flake the salmon into a bowl and set aside.

Melt the butter in a clean saucepan and sauté the chopped onion until soft; then put with the flaked salmon. Then add the chopped egg, grated rind and juice of the limes and lemon, cayenne pepper, paprika, chopped parsley and sea salt to taste. When the rice has cooked add to the kedgeree mixture blending well with a metal spoon (a wooden spoon breaks up the rice too much). Fold in the cream and mix well, remove and serve.

Pan-Fried Salmon with Bacon and Pea Purée

A birr; a whirr; a salmon's on,
A goodly fish; a thumper:
Bring up; bring up the ready gaff,
And if we land him we shall quaff a bumper.

(*The Taking of the Salmon*, Thomas Todd-Stoddart)

Salmon is reputed to be one of our most highly regarded fish, specifically the ones caught early in the season. These tend to have the finest flavour. They can be expensive to buy but as the season progresses, the price does come down. Those fortunate enough to fish the rivers and lochs of Scotland will be amply rewarded for their efforts if successful in landing a good-sized, glistening, silver scaled wild Scottish salmon and will have fully deserved their 'bumper'.

Ingredients to serve 2

250 g (9 oz) frozen peas
4-tablespoons double cream
A little grated nutmeg to taste
Sea salt and ground black pepper

6 rashers, streaky bacon
2 salmon fillets, skin and any bones removed
1 level tablespoon chopped parsley

Method

Cook the peas in a little water until soft, drain and put them into a food processor. Add the cream, grated nutmeg and season to taste and blend to a smooth thick purée. Transfer the purée to a basin and keep warm until required.

Fry the bacon until just beginning to brown; remove from the pan.

Fry the salmon in the bacon fat, brown on both sides. Put the pea purée into a saucepan and heat through. Divide the purée equally between two warm plates; lay the salmon on top then lay the bacon on top of the fish. Sprinkle over the chopped parsley and serve.

Pan-Fried Trout with Roasted Rhubarb

Rhubarb, once the staple pudding of Victorian nurseries and school meals has given rhubarb its poor image, but because of its abundance of vitamin C and its 'good for you' character, it has remained, despite constant stewing, firmly on English menus. A train called the 'Pink Express' used to run nightly from Yorkshire with crates of rhubarb destined for the dining tables of London.

It is still grown today in Yorkshire in low, long dark sheds known as rhubarb 'cathedrals', lit entirely by candles.

This recipe lifts rhubarb from being just a pie filling to a delicious, unusual, piquant vegetable accompaniment, that will surprise friends and family. But, do use very young, thin-stemmed, pink 'forced' rhubarb, it is less acidic and has a more delicate flavour than the main crop.

Ingredients to serve 4

8 sticks young rhubarb, washed and cut into
  chunks
Olive oil for drizzling, frying and roasting
Sea salt and freshly ground black pepper

4 red peppers
4 fillets fresh trout, skin and any bones
  removed

Method

Pre-heat the oven to 200ºC/400ºF/gas mark 6. Lay the rhubarb pieces in a roasting dish, drizzle over a little olive oil; season with sea salt and black pepper. Cut the peppers in half, remove the stalk, core and seed. Lay them cut side down on a separate baking tray, brush over with olive oil and roast in the oven uncovered, along with the rhubarb for approximately 15–20 minutes until the skin of the pepper 'blisters'. Remove from the oven and peel away the pepper skin.

Heat a tablespoon of olive oil in a frying pan and pan-fry the trout fillets for approximately 5 minutes on both sides until crisp, brown and cooked through. Serve with the roast rhubarb, roast peppers and minted new potatoes.

Salmon with Tomato and Vanilla Mirepoix

A gourmet fisherman when asked which piece of the salmon he would like, he replied: 'The tail end, starting just behind the gills.'

(*Pass the Port,* Viscount Fitzharris)

Ingredients to serve 4

125 ml (4 fl oz) vegetable oil

2 large shallots, peeled and finely chopped

8 tomatoes, skinned and chopped

$^1/_2$ vanilla pod, split into two lengthways

1 teaspoon caster sugar

4 fresh salmon fillets, skin and any bones removed

Sea salt and freshly ground black pepper

A little chopped fresh parsley to garnish

8 asparagus spears, cooked

For the sauce

Good handful of fresh chives, chopped

150 ml ($^1/_4$ pint) single cream

70 g (2$^1/_2$ oz) unsalted butter

175 ml (6 fl oz) milk

Salt and pepper

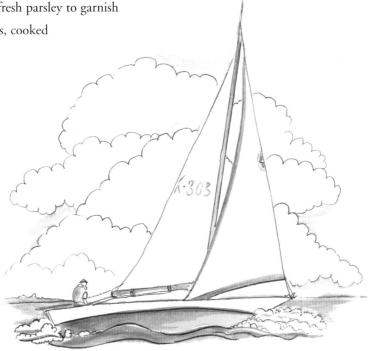

Method

Heat the oil in a frying pan and lightly sauté the shallots until soft. Add the tomatoes. Scrape the vanilla seeds from the pods into the tomato, then put the pods themselves and the sugar into the shallot and tomato mixture. Cook over a very low heat for a few moments to dissolve the sugar.

Remove from the heat and take out the vanilla pods. Set the tomato and vanilla mirepoix aside.

Put the salmon into a steamer, season with a little sea salt and black pepper; steam for 5 minutes. The exact time will depend on the thickness of the fillets. Test by gently pulling apart the thickest part of the fillet – if it still looks raw, steam for a little longer, but take care not to overcook.

To make the sauce Put the chives, cream, butter, milk and seasonings into a small saucepan and bring to simmering point stirring for a couple of minutes. Remove from the heat.

Gently warm the tomato and vanilla mirepoix. Place a fillet of cooked salmon onto warm dinner plates. Mound a spoonful of the mirepoix on top of each fillet, pour the sauce around the salmon and sprinkle over a little chopped parsley. Finally, arrange 2 asparagus spears alongside each of the salmon fillets. Serve with creamed potatoes and steamed baby spinach.

Smoked Mackerel Pâté

A quick and easy pâté made in minutes, perfect as a speedy starter served with fingers of toast or warm oatcakes; spread on hot toast it's great for breakfast as a fishy alternative to kippers.

Ingredients to serve 4

4 smoked mackerel fillets
70 g (2½ oz) softened butter
4 tablespoons double cream
Cayenne pepper to taste
Juice and grated rind of 1 lemon

Method

Put all ingredients into a food processor and blend until smooth. Transfer to a bowl, cover with cling film and keep in the refrigerator until required. Pâté should keep for 4–5 days in the refrigerator.

Trout Mousse with Watercress Mayonnaise

It is a pleasant, leisurely, business – this after-tea fishing. If you are fortunate, you may get all your letters written beforehand: and if you are very fortunate, you may even have paid all your bills. But before setting out a most important thing is to be sure that others will not wait dinner, to insist that a bit of cold meat, bread and cheese is all you require. If you feel at any time during the walk that you must hurry, then your evening is spoilt.

(*English Sport*, Captain H. F. H. Hardy)

A very simple dish to make, ideal for a cold supper or light lunch; also good for picnics being easily transportable.

Ingredients to serve 4–6

85 g (3 oz) butter
70 g (2¹/₂ oz) plain flour
300 ml (¹/₂ pint) whole milk
1 sprig fresh dill or fennel, chopped
1 tablespoon anchovy essence
2 teaspoons tomato paste
Juice of ¹/₂ lemon
2 tablespoons Amontillado sherry
4 sheets leaf gelatine, soaked in a little cold
    water
450 g (1 lb) cooked trout, cleaned, skin and
    bones removed
125 ml (4 fl oz) double cream

For the mayonnaise

300 ml (¹/₂ pint) made mayonnaise
Sea salt and black pepper to taste
Bunch of watercress, washed, stalks and any
    yellow leaves removed

To garnish

Slices of lemon and small sprigs of watercress

Method

Melt the butter in a saucepan, add the flour, cook and stir for 3 minutes. Remove from the heat and gradually blend in the milk, then return to the heat and cook for a further 2 minutes until thickened. Remove from the heat and mix in the chopped dill or fennel, anchovy essence, tomato paste, lemon juice, sherry and the drained floppy gelatine. Blend well together. Allow the mousse mixture to cool a little.

Flake the trout and put into a food processor, add the cooled mousse mixture and whiz briefly. Tip out into a bowl. Lightly whisk the cream until just holding its shape and then fold into the cooled trout mousse mixture. Spoon into individual pots or one large dish, cover and leave to set in the refrigerator.

To make the watercress mayonnaise Reserve a few sprigs of watercress for garnishing; put the remaining watercress in a food processor. Add the mayonnaise and seasonings and whiz together until smooth.

When required, decorate the mousse with twists of fresh lemon and a sprig of watercress. Alternatively, dip the containers quickly into a little boiling water to release the mousse. If still reluctant to come out of the pot, run a knife round the edge of the mousse to loosen. Turn out onto a plate and decorate with sprigs of watercress and slices of lemon. Serve with the mayonnaise.

MAIN COURSES

Beef Fillets in a Smoked Ham Sauce

Ingredients to serve 4

1 teaspoon crushed black peppercorns

4 beef fillet steaks (approx 125 g / 4^1/$_2$ oz for
  each steak)

2–3 tablespoons chilli oil (or oil of your
choice)

For the sauce

1 tablespoon olive oil

6 shallots, peeled and finely chopped

1 tablespoon plain flour

300 ml (^{1}/$_2$ pint) beef or vegetable stock

2 tablespoons brandy

2 teaspoons Dijon mustard

Sea salt to taste

115 g (4 oz) cooked sliced smoked ham, cut
  into strips

150 ml (5 fl oz) single cream

Method

To make the sauce Put the oil into a saucepan and add the chopped shallots, cook until
soft. Stir in the flour and cook for a few minutes to cook the flour. Pour in the stock,
add the brandy, mustard and salt to taste. Simmer until reduced by two-thirds. When
reduced, put in two-thirds of the ham, stir and put to one side.

For the fillets Press the crushed peppercorns evenly onto the fillets. Heat the oil in a frying
pan and sauté the fillets to your liking. Keep the steaks warm while you return the sauce
to the heat, add the cream, reheat gently but do not boil. Pour the sauce over the fillets
and scatter the remaining strips of ham over each steak.

Brandied Lamb

Mrs Beeton informs us in her instructive publication *Household Management* that sheep and lamb bones, when burnt, produce an 'animal charcoal' – ivory black – to polish the boots of the country squire or farmer; the skin, when split, provides a 'housing' for his horse, a mat for his carriage or a lining for his hat.

The secret of this recipe is in the sauce, the flavour coming from the flambéed lamb juices, brandy and the tasty residue from the roasting pan.

Ingredients to serve 6–8

1 large leg of lamb	40 g (1½ oz) unsalted butter
1 sprig fresh rosemary	40 g (1½ oz) plain flour
1 tin condensed consommé	1 tablespoon chopped chives
175 ml (6 fl oz) dry white wine	1 tablespoon clear honey
Sea salt and freshly ground black pepper to taste	100 ml (3½ fl oz) brandy
	150 ml (¼ pint) double cream

Method

Pre-heat the oven to 190ºC/375ºF/gas mark 5. Place the lamb in a roasting tin with the sprig of rosemary; pour over the consommé, white wine and season to taste. Roast in the centre of the pre-heated oven for 1½ –2 hours. When the lamb is cooked through, remove from the oven and, holding the lamb with a fork, tip the meat juices into a basin. Reserve for the sauce. Reduce the oven temperature to 150ºC/300ºF/gas mark 2 and return the lamb to the oven.

Skim any fat from the top of the meat juices and discard the fat.

Melt the butter in a saucepan, add the flour and cook for 2 minutes, stirring all the time. Remove from the heat and stir in the meat juices. Return to the heat and cook until the sauce begins to thicken. If too thick, slacken with a little water to your preferred consistency. Add the chives and honey to the sauce and keep warm.

Heat the brandy in a small saucepan. When hot, remove the lamb from the oven and pour over the hot brandy and set alight to burn off the alcohol. Put the lamb onto a warm serving dish. Add a little water to the roasting tin, deglaze the pan by stirring round and scraping up all the meaty residue, pour into the sauce, add the cream and check seasonings.

Pour the sauce over the slices of lamb or serve separately in a warm sauce boat.

Pork Tenderloin with Spring Herb Stuffing

Charles and Tom Palmer walked over from Eardisley to see me. The day was bitterly cold with a cruel east wind and whilst they were here a wild snowstorm came on.

(Kilvert's Diary, 30 March 1878)

This sounds like a fairly typical spring day when no sport is to be had, but is just right for staying home and enjoying lunch or dinner with friends.

Ingredients to serve 4–6

35 g (1¼ oz)unsalted butter
1 small onion, peeled and chopped
5 rashers rindless, streaky bacon
100 g (3½ oz) fresh wholemeal breadcrumbs
Grated rind of 1 small lemon
1 tablespoon thyme leaves, freshly chopped
½ tablespoon chopped chives
1 small egg, beaten
Sea salt and freshly ground black pepper to taste
2 pork tenderloins, trimmed, flattened between cling film
1 tablespoon chopped fresh parsley to garnish

For the gravy

2 teaspoons cornflour mixed with 4 tablespoons water
1 teaspoon fresh tarragon, chopped
1 teaspoon Dijon mustard
125 ml (4 fl oz) double cream

Method

Melt the butter in a saucepan, put in the onion and cook until soft. Chop 3 bacon rashers into small pieces and add to the onion. Cook for 3 minutes. Transfer the sautéed onion and bacon into a mixing bowl; add the breadcrumbs, lemon rind, thyme, chives and egg and season to taste. Blend and bind well together.

Pre-heat the oven to 160ºC/325ºF/gas mark 3. Take the pieces of flattened tenderloin and lay the stuffing mixture down the centre of each. Season again to taste and roll up into a 'sausage' shape. Tie with string or secure with a skewer. Put the stuffed tenderloins into an ovenproof dish and lay a rasher of bacon over the full length of each one, and cook in the pre-heated oven for 1 hour or until the meat is tender. When cooked, remove from the oven and transfer the tenderloins onto a warm serving dish, reserving the juices for the gravy.

To make the gravy Pour the meat juices into a saucepan, add the slackened cornflour, and stir over a moderate heat until thickened. Mix in the tarragon, mustard and cream.

Carve the tenderloins into slices, not too thin or the stuffing will fall out. Arrange on dinner plates, pour over the sauce and sprinkle with chopped parsley.

Breaded Chicken Breasts with Basil and Goat's Cheese

In a cold, dark medieval night, groping for a fowl to cook for supper, you were instructed to take one roosting next to the cock – she was sure to be the fattest.

(Food in England, Dorothy Hartley)

Ingredients to serve 4

4 skinless chicken breasts

115 g (4 oz) soft goat's cheese

8–12 large basil leaves

Sea salt and freshly ground black pepper

2 tablespoons plain flour seasoned with salt and pepper

1 egg, beaten

115 g (4 oz) fresh breadcrumbs

Method

Make an incision in the thickest part of each chicken breast. Cut the goat's cheese into four and wrap each piece with basil leaves. Season the chicken to taste and push a portion of goat's cheese and basil into the incision of each chicken breast. Secure with a cocktail stick or small skewer. Coat each chicken breast with the seasoned flour, dip into the beaten egg and then coat with the breadcrumbs. Chill in the refrigerator until required.

When ready to eat, deep-fry in hot oil for 15–20 minutes depending on size and thickness of chicken breasts. Remove the cocktail stick or skewer before serving.

Chicken with Prawn Sauce

Few persons bestow half as much attention on the preservation of their own health, as they daily devote to that of their dogs and horses.

(*The Cook's Oracle*, Dr William Kitchiner)

Don't be put off by the unusual combination of meat and fish; it is very tasty. Elizabethans were fond of putting fish, meat and fruit together in the same dish, as still happens today with anchovy essence going into the making of Melton Mowbray pork pies.

Ingredients to serve 4

40 g (1$^1/_2$ oz) butter

4 free-range chicken breasts, skin left on

4 shallots, peeled and chopped

40 g (1$^1/_2$ oz) plain flour

150 ml ($^1/_4$ pint) chicken or vegetables stick

100 ml (3$^1/_2$ fl oz) white wine

2 rounded teaspoons tomato paste

Sea salt and freshly ground black pepper to
  taste

150 ml ($^1/_4$ pint) single or double cream

115 g (4 oz) fresh or frozen cooked prawns

2 tablespoons parsley, freshly chopped

Method

Melt the butter in a saucepan and seal the chicken breasts until just turning brown. Remove from the pan and put into a large heavy-based saucepan with a lid.

Put the chopped onion into the pan and fry until just turning soft and then stir in the flour. Cook for 3 minutes and then pour in the stock, stir well and then add the wine, tomato paste. Season to taste and then pour over the chicken, put on the lid and cook for 15–20 minutes until the chicken is tender. When the chicken is cooked, remove from the saucepan and keep warm. Boil the liquid in the pan until reduced slightly then stir in the cream. Check the seasonings and finally add the prawns. Return the chicken to the pan and re-heat to serve, but do not overheat or the prawns will become tough. Scatter over chopped parsley to serve.

Spicy Roast Chicken with Roast Vine Tomatoes

Ingredients to serve 2

2 free-range, boneless chicken breasts

1 level teaspoon cayenne pepper (optional)

4 teaspoons crunchy honey mustard

6–8 medium vine tomatoes, washed

4 tablespoons olive oil

2 tablespoons chopped basil and thyme, mixed

Method

Pre-heat the oven to 175ºC/350ºF/gas mark 4 Open out the chicken breasts by slicing in half but not all the way through. Once opened out, the chicken breast can be flattened out: it should look roughly heart-shaped. Place the prepared chicken into a roasting tin leaving space for tomatoes. Mix the cayenne pepper if used with the mustard and spread evenly over each piece of chicken.

Lay the tomatoes, still on the vine, next to the chicken, drizzle over the olive oil, sprinkle the chopped herbs over the tomatoes. Put in the pre-heated oven. Roast for approximately 10–15 minutes depending on the thickness of the chicken breast. When thoroughly cooked, remove from the oven and serve with small boiled potatoes or new ones, tossed in olive oil and turmeric.

Cook's note
The chicken can be grilled if you prefer.

Sautéed Liver with a Port and Orange Sauce

Nimrod tells us that 'Mad' Jack Mytton of Halston, Shropshire, drank from four to six bottles of port daily. The question of how he consumed this quantity is answered easily, Nimrod continues. 'He (Mytton) shaved with a bottle of it on his toilet; he worked steadily at it throughout the day, by a glass or two at a time, and at least a bottle with his luncheon; and the after dinner and after supper work – not losing sight of it in the billiard room – completed the Herculean task.'

(The Life of John Mytton, Nimrod, 1827)

I rather think that this dish would have gone down very well at Halston, providing that the cook could rescue a little port from the sideboard. We trust you will not have that problem.

Ingredients to serve 4

500 g (1 lb 2 oz) lambs liver, membrane and
  tubes removed if necessary
2 tablespoons plain flour seasoned with a
  little salt
25 g (1 oz) butter
2 tablespoons olive oil

Juice and rind of 2 small oranges
4 tablespoons tawny port
125 ml (4 fl oz) beef stock
2 teaspoons redcurrant jelly
1 tablespoon chopped chives
Sea salt and pepper to taste

Method

Cut the liver evenly into slices and toss in the seasoned flour. Melt the butter with the oil in a frying pan and sauté the pieces of liver. For soft, velvety texture to the liver, take care not to over-cook. Remove from the pan and keep warm. Add all the remaining ingredients to the frying pan and cook until reduced slightly. Check the seasonings, return the liver to the pan, stir and re-heat gently if necessary, and serve.

Venison and Mushroom Carbonade

Ingredients to serve 6–8

Vegetable oil for browning meat

900 g (2 lb) stewing venison, cut into chunks

125 g (4 oz) streaky bacon, cut into small
  pieces

2 medium onions, peeled and chopped

1 clove garlic, crushed

2 heaped tablespoons plain flour

568 ml (19 fl oz) dark beer

1 tin condensed consommé

2 teaspoons tomato paste

2 tablespoons redcurrant jelly

Sea salt and ground black pepper

250 g (9 oz) button mushrooms, wiped and
  quartered

1 tablespoon fresh thyme, chopped

Method

Heat the oil in a large frying pan and brown the venison a small batch at a time. When evenly browned, put into a casserole. Fry the bacon pieces and add to the casserole. Fry the onion until just turning brown, add the garlic, stir briefly and add to the casserole. Put the flour into the pan and cook for 2–3 minutes, pour in the beer and stir well. Add the consommé, tomato paste, redcurrant jelly and seasonings then bring to the boil. Pour the boiling sauce over the venison, scatter in the mushrooms and chopped thyme. Cook in the oven at 170ºC/325ºF/gas mark 3 for 2¹/₂–3 hours.

Serving suggestion Celeriac and potato mash or jacket potatoes

PUDDINGS

Beaver Hat Pudding

Squire, farmer, stage-coachman, innkeeper, traveller, labourer, gamekeeper, tinker, tailor, butcher, baker and candlestick maker–all wore the beaver hat. They wore it in love and in sport, in travel, and of course to church. They went shooting in it, they hunted in it, and fished and played cricket in it; and the only time they discarded it was when they went up to bed – when they always put on a nightcap in case their heads should miss it.

(The Romance of the Road, Cecil Aldin)

This delicious sponge pudding separates when cooking to give its own sauce. When the pudding is cooked and turned out for serving a good deep dish is necessary to catch the sauce.

Ingredients to serve 4–6

170 g (6 oz) butter

250 g (9 oz) soft brown sugar

3 eggs, beaten

125 g (4$^{1}/_{2}$ oz) chocolate, melted in a basin over hot water

70 g (2$^{1}/_{2}$ oz) chopped walnuts (optional)

225 g (8 oz) self-raising flour

1$^{1}/_{2}$ teaspoons baking powder

450 ml ($^{3}/_{4}$ pint) milk

Method

Pre-heat the oven to 170ºC/325ºF/gas mark 3. Beat the butter and two-thirds of the sugar together. Beat in the egg and then beat in the melted chocolate. Stir in the walnuts if using. Sift together the flour and baking powder and fold into the cake mixture and then pour into a greased ovenproof dish. Mix together the remaining sugar with the milk and pour over the sponge mixture. Put into the pre-heated oven and bake for 1 hour 15 minutes until the pudding is spongy to the touch. If you wish to turn the pudding out, run a knife around the edge of the pudding to loosen and turn out onto a deep plate, otherwise spoon straight from the dish not forgetting to dig deep to get at the sauce.

Cook's note
Check the sponge after an hour as some ovens run hotter than others.

Chocolate Mint Mousse

This mousse is especially good for an 'at home' day: very rich, dark and comforting.

Ingredients to serve 4–6

250 g (9 oz) dark chocolate

3 tablespoons water

60 g (2¼ oz) unsalted butter

4 teaspoons coffee essence (extract)

2 teaspoons peppermint essence (extract)

3 eggs, separated

100 ml (3½ fl oz) whipping cream

4–6 fresh mint leaves (optional)

4–6 chocolate mints for decoration (optional)

Method

Break the chocolate into small pieces, put into a basin and add the water, butter, coffee and peppermint. Stand the basin over a pan of hot water (the water should not touch the bottom of the basin – if it does, it will over cook the chocolate). Stir thoroughly until the mixture is free of lumps and thick and glossy. Whisk in the egg yolks one at a time (this must be done over the heat). When completely blended, remove the basin from the heat and allow the mixture to cool. When the mixture has cooled, whip the cream and fold into the mousse mixture. Whisk the egg whites until just holding shape and fold into the chocolate mousse. Put into serving pots, cover and chill in the refrigerator until required. Remove from the refrigerator half an hour before serving, so the mousse will not be too solid. Decorate with a fresh mint leaf and a chocolate mint if desired.

Gooseberry and Honey Pie

That thither all the season did pursue
Wi' mellow goosberrys of every hue

(*The Shepherd's Calendar*, John Clare)

Gooseberries are one of the first fruits of spring and one which grows prolifically in old cottage or farmhouse kitchen gardens. It was favoured not just because it was easy to grow, but also for its versatility in cooking – in savoury as well as sweet dishes. Adding honey, offsets the tartness of the gooseberry: more or less honey can be added according to preference.

Ingredients to serve 4–6

750 g (1 lb 10 oz) gooseberries, washed, topped and tailed
60 g (2¼ oz) unsalted butter
4 tablespoons fresh orange juice
3 tablespoons honey

250 g (9 oz) prepared shortcrust pastry
A little milk to glaze
A teaspoon of golden granulated sugar for sprinkling

Method

Pre-heat the oven to 220ºC/425ºF/gas mark 7. Place a pie funnel in the centre of a deep pie dish, fill the dish with gooseberries and dot the fruit with the butter. Pour in the orange juice and spoon in the honey.

Roll the pastry to form a lid. Moisten the rim of the dish, cut a strip of pastry from the rolled lid and press the strip around the edge of the pie dish. Lay the pastry lid over the top and, with finger and thumb, press to 'flute' the edges to seal the pie. Brush the lid with the milk. Sprinkle over the sugar and bake in the pre-heated oven for 20 minutes to cook the pastry, then reduce the temperature to 200ºC/400ºF/gas mark 6 and cook for a further 20 minutes. When cooked, remove from the oven, sprinkle over a little extra sugar if desired and serve with clotted or double cream.

Horse's Neck Syllabub

…there is nothing more cheering to the spirits, than the sight of Newmarket Heath on a fine, fresh spring morning like the present. The wind seems to go by you at a racing pace, and the blood canters up and down the veins with the finest and freest action imaginable.

(Jorrock's Jaunts and Jollities, R. S. Surtees)

'Horse's neck' is a naval term for the drink, brandy and ginger, much enjoyed by naval officers in the wardrooms of the Royal Navy, the ginger being ginger ale, not ginger wine.

Ingredients to serve 4

300 ml ($^1/_2$ pint) double cream
125 ml (4 fl oz) ginger wine
Juice of $^1/_2$ lemon
Clear honey to taste
4–5 tablespoons brandy
A few pieces of preserved ginger, sliced

Method

Whip the cream until it just holds its shape. Mix together the wine, lemon juice, honey and brandy and then gradually whisk into the cream. Pour into individual glasses and top each glass with a couple of pieces of preserved ginger. Refrigerate until required.

Cook's note
Brandy snaps can be crumbled on top instead of preserved ginger if preferred.

Old English Sherry Trifle

Give me sacke, old sacke, boys,
To make the muses merry.
The life of mirth and the joy of the earth
Is a cup of good old sherry.

(Ballad from Pasquil's Palinodia, in *Inns, Ales, and drinking Customs of old England*, F. W. Hackward)

Ingredients to serve 8–10

For the trifle

500 g (1 lb 2 oz) Madeira sponge cake

2–3 tablespoons raspberry or strawberry jam
  (homemade if possible)

100 ml (3^1/$_2$ fl oz) Amontillado sherry

4 tablespoons brandy (optional)

250 g (9 oz) frozen raspberries
  (defrosted – reserving the juice)

115 g (4 oz) toasted flaked almonds

For the custard topping

400 ml (13 fl oz) whole milk

^{1}/$_2$ vanilla pod, split

3 tablespoons caster sugar

4 egg yolks

125 ml double cream

3 tablespoons of caster sugar

4 sheets leaf gelatine, soaked in a little cold
  water

300 ml (^{1}/$_2$ pint) whipping cream for the
  topping

A little caster sugar for sweetening the
  cream (optional)

Method

Heat the milk with the vanilla pod, remove from the heat and allow to infuse for 20 minutes

Cut the sponge cake into thick slices. Spread each slice with the jam and lay in the bottom of a large, glass serving bowl. Pour in the sherry and brandy if used. Spoon over the raspberries with its juice, and scatter half the amount of toasted almonds over the raspberries.

To make the custard Whisk the egg yolks until thick and creamy. Remove the vanilla pod from the milk, scrape the vanilla seeds into the egg mixture and pour in the infused milk. Pour the custard into a saucepan and heat gently, stirring constantly until it begins to thicken, then remove from the heat. Drop the soaked gelatine leaves into the custard and whisk until dissolved. Allow to cool by standing the saucepan in a bowl of iced water to speed up the cooling process. Whisk the double cream until it just holds its shape and fold into the cooled custard, then pour the custard over the trifle. Cover and allow to set in the refrigerator.

When ready to serve, whisk the whipping cream, sweeten with a little sugar if desired, spread over the set custard, then scatter over the remaining toasted almonds.

Queen of Puddings

A sporting young man and his elderly mother from the country were attending a race meeting; it was the old lady's first experience of racing. 'I say mother,' said the young man, 'I've been wondering for ages what's in that bulky parcel you're carrying.' 'Well,' said the old lady, 'in your letter you said to bring something to put on the horses … so I bought this old eiderdown, I hope it isn't too shabby.'

(*Sporting and Dramatic Yarns*, R. J. B. Sellar)

Elderly mothers may not be too conversant with the jargon of horse-racing, but they would certainly be familiar with this spectacular, golden-brown topped pudding. Despite its impressive appearance and aristocratic title, it is very easy to make.

Ingredients to serve 4–6

150 g (5^1/$_2$ oz) fine white breadcrumbs
55 g (2 oz) caster sugar
Grated rind of 1 lemon
600 ml (1 pint) whole milk
55 g (2 oz) unsalted butter
4 large egg yolks
3 tablespoons raspberry or strawberry jam

For the topping
4 egg whites
170 g (6 oz) caster sugar

Method

Mix together the breadcrumbs, sugar and lemon rind. Pour the milk into a saucepan and heat until just warm. Put the butter into the milk to melt, whisk in the egg yolks and pour over the breadcrumb mixture. Put the mixture into a dish and leave for 30 minutes to allow the breadcrumbs to swell in the milk. After that time, bake in the oven for 30 minutes at 180ºC/350ºF/gas mark 4. The top should be firm to the touch when ready. Remove from the oven and when the mixture has set, spread the jam evenly over the top taking care not to break the surface crust.

To make the topping Beat the egg whites until very stiff, gradually whisking in the sugar, a spoon at a time. Keep whisking until all the sugar is thoroughly blended in. Spread the meringue over the jam and with a fork, bring the meringue into 'peaks'. Dust over a little more sugar, turn down the oven to 150ºC/300ºF/gas mark 2 and return the pudding to the oven for 10–15 minutes until the meringue is crisp and golden.

CAKES

Connemara Chocolate Cake

A great cake for tea-time at the races to celebrate St Patrick's Day or if you've been fortunate enough to back a winner. The recipe is for two cakes which can be served separately or sandwiched together with double cream.

Ingredients for 2 cakes

Softened butter for greasing cake tins

115 g (4 oz) vegetable fat

250 g (9 oz) caster sugar

55 g (2 oz) dark chocolate, broken into pieces

200 ml (7 fl oz) water

25 g (1 oz) cocoa powder

170 g (6 oz) plain flour

$^1/_4$ teaspoon baking powder

1 teaspoon bicarbonate of soda

2 eggs, beaten

For the icing (optional)

115 g (4 oz) icing sugar, sifted

2 teaspoons cocoa powder mixed with 4 tablespoons warm water

Method

Pre-heat the oven to 180ºC/350ºF/gas mark 4. Grease two 20-cm (8-inch) cake tins and line the base with baking parchment.

Cream together the fat and sugar until light and fluffy – this can be done in a food blender if desired.

Put the pieces of chocolate into a small saucepan with the water and dissolve over a low heat. When the chocolate has dissolved, whisk in the cocoa powder until well blended and free from lumps. Remove from the heat and cool.

Sift into a bowl the flour, baking powder and bicarbonate of soda.

Beat the eggs into the fat and sugar mixture, then fold in the sifted flour a little at a time, alternating with the melted chocolate. Blend well together so there are no dry patches. Divide the cake mixture between the two tins. Bake in the pre-heated oven for 35 minutes, until the top is springy to the touch. Remove from the oven and cool slightly before removing onto a wire rack to cool completely.

Prepare the chocolate topping Mix the sugar and slackened cocoa powder together to a smooth paste. Spread evenly on top of the cake if sandwiching together, or both cakes if single.

Dark Rum Butter Cake

Gobble, gobble, gobble, was the order of the day.

(*Mr Sponge's Sporting Tour*, R. S. Surtees)

Ingredients to serve 4–6

200 g (7 oz) soft brown sugar

170 g (6 oz) unsalted butter

5 medium eggs

Grated rind and juice of 1 small orange

Grated rind and juice of 1 small lemon

4 tablespoons dark rum

85 g (3 oz) semolina

250 g (9 oz) self-raising flour

1 teaspoon baking powder

Method

Pre-heat the oven to 190ºC/375ºF/gas mark 5. Grease 1 kg (2 lb) loaf tin and line the bottom with greaseproof paper.

Put the sugar and butter into a food processor, cream together until pale and creamy and then one at a time, add the eggs, blending as you go. Add the rind and juice of the orange and lemon, pour in the rum. Sift together the semolina, flour and baking powder and tip into the food processor. Blend to mix all the ingredients together. Pour the mixture into the prepared loaf tin. Bake in the pre-heated oven for ³/₄ hour, then turn down the temperature to 180ºC/350ºF/gas mark 4 and continue to bake for 15–30 minutes more. If the top is turning too brown too quickly, rest a piece of kitchen foil over the top. When cooked, turn out onto a wire rack to cool.

Irish Whiskey Lemon Cake

The first delicate pangs of hunger were stealing upon us, and I felt reasonably certain that nothing necessary to our welfare had been forgotten. I lit a cigarette and pulled my cap over my eyes and listened to a lark, while my wife clattered in the luncheon basket.

(*In Mr Knox's Country*, E. OE. Somerville and Martin Ross)

Ingredients to serve 4–6

170 g (6 oz) sultanas
6 tablespoons Irish whiskey
Grated rind and juice of 1 large lemon
170 g (6 oz) butter softened
170 g (6 oz) caster sugar
3 eggs, separated

115 g (4 oz) self-raising flour sifted with 1
  teaspoon baking powder
70 g (2$^1/_2$ oz) ground almonds

For the topping (optional)

1 tablespoon lemon juice
A little whiskey to mix
115 g (4 oz) icing sugar

Method

Pre-heat the oven to 160ºC/325ºF/gas mark 3. Grease a 20 cm (8 inch) square cake tin and line with greaseproof paper.

Into a bowl put the sultanas, whiskey, lemon rind and juice, leave to infuse. Cream the butter and sugar together until fluffy and light. Beat in the egg yolks one at a time. Add the soaked sultanas, lemon juice and whiskey and a spoonful of the flour; mix well together. Fold in the ground almonds and then fold in the remaining flour. Whisk the egg whites until stiff and fold into the cake mixture; take care not to over mix. Turn the mixture into the prepared cake tin and bake in the pre-heated oven for 1$^1/_2$ hours until firm to the touch. Test after 1 hour. Cool the cake on a wire rack.

For the topping Mix the lemon juice, whiskey and icing sugar until it is a coating consistency, then spread over the top of the cake.

Summer

SOUPS

Chilled Curried Apple Soup

After Goodwood came Cowes Week, and Cowes Roads were filled to overflowing with every description of craft. It was a glorious sight to see the big racing yachts come swooping down the Solent with every stitch of canvas set. My mother and I often stayed at Eaglehurst with Count and Countess Batthyany. They lived in foreign style; we lunched and dined at small tables in the garden, which in the evening was lit up by Chinese lanterns. The view of the sea and the twinkling lights from the yachts made a lovely picture in the moonlight.

(*Chit-Chat*, Lady Augusta Fane)

What a perfect setting for a summer lunch or dinner party. This chilled soup is ideal for just such an occasion. Using coconut milk imparts a delicious underlying flavour, complimenting the curry paste perfectly.

Ingredients to serve 4–6

3 tablespoons vegetable oil

2 medium onions, peeled and chopped

1 crushed clove garlic

900 g (2 lb) eating apples, peeled, cored and sliced

3 teaspoons curry paste

Juice of 1 small lemon

750 ml (1$^{1}/_{4}$ pints) chicken stock

2 teaspoons mango chutney

225 g (8 fl oz) coconut milk

125 ml (4 fl oz) Greek yoghurt

Sea salt and freshly ground black pepper to taste

Double cream to garnish

Method

Heat the oil in a large saucepan, add the onion, garlic and chopped apple; cover and 'sweat' until the onion and apple slices are soft; stir from time to time to prevent sticking. Mix in the curry paste, lemon juice and stock. Simmer for 20 minutes until all ingredients are well blended. Add the chutney, stir well and remove from the heat. Allow to cool and then put into a food processor. Blend until smooth then whisk in the coconut milk, yoghurt, salt and pepper to taste. Pour into a suitable container and chill in the refrigerator until required. When ready to serve, pour into chilled soup bowls and swirl a spoonful of double cream on top.

Crab Soup

Devilish good dinner – cold, but capital
(Dingley Dell and Muggleton Cricket Dinner, at the Blue Lion Inn,
Muggleton, Pickwick Papers, Charles Dickens)

This is such an easy recipe and can be made in advance. It can also be served hot for a special occasion such as Cross Country Day at the Badminton Horse Trials, or served cold whilst watching a polo match on a warm summer's day.

Ingredients to serve 4–6

40 g (1¹/₂ oz) butter

1 medium onion, peeled and finely chopped

1 bay leaf

1 crushed clove garlic

900 g (2 lb) tomatoes, skinned

1 tablespoon tomato purée

1 litre (1³/₄ pints) chicken stock

3 teaspoons anchovy essence

1 dressed crab, brown and white meat

Grated rind and juice of 1 lemon

150 ml (¹/₄ pint) double cream

Method

Melt the butter in a saucepan, add the onion and cook until soft and then add the bay leaf, garlic and tomatoes. Cover, and cook until the tomatoes are soft and pulpy. Stir in the tomato purée, stock and anchovy essence, then simmer for 10–15 minutes.

Remove any pieces of shell from the crab meat, separate the white meat from the brown. Put the brown meat into the soup mixture and add the lemon rind and juice. Transfer to a food processor and liquidise until smooth. Return the soup to a clean saucepan, stir in the cream and white crab meat, and chill until required.

Cook's note
The soup chills faster in a metal saucepan.

Chilled Cucumber and Lovage Soup

Scottish Highlanders used to chew on lovage as a substitute for tobacco. It was also believed to keep away colds which could be why lovage was so popular in the old herb gardens. It is well worth growing or seeking out today for its aromatic, celery flavour which enhances soups, stews and salads.

   This summer soup is very quick to prepare, with everything going into one bowl and blended together.

Ingredients to serve 4–6

1 medium sized white onion, peeled and finely chopped

1 small crushed clove garlic

1 large or 2 small cucumbers, peeled and chopped

2 large sprigs lovage leaves, washed and cut into pieces

150 g (5$^1/_2$ oz) natural yoghurt

900 ml (1$^1/_2$ pints) chicken or vegetable stock

Sea salt and white pepper to taste

Method

Put all ingredients into a large bowl and mix well together. Liquidise one third of the mixture at a time until smooth and creamy.

   Pour into soup bowls and decorate the top with a fresh lovage leaf and a thin slice of cucumber.

   For transportation, pour into a vacuum flask with one or two ice cubes (not too many or the ice will dilute the soup).

Chilled Curried Mango Soup

Ingredients to serve 4–6

125 ml (4 fl oz) vegetable oil

2 medium onions, peeled and finely chopped

4 eating apples, peeled, cored and chopped

900 ml (1$\frac{1}{2}$ pints) apple juice

3 ripe mangoes, skinned, stoned and chopped

Juice of 2 lemons

3 teaspoons mango chutney

Salt and freshly ground white pepper

175 ml (6 fl oz) Greek yoghurt or single cream

Method

Put the oil into a saucepan, add the onion and apple and cook gently until soft but not brown. Pour in the apple juice and simmer for 10 minutes. Remove from the heat and add the mango, lemon juice, curry paste, mango chutney and seasonings. Liquidise the soup a little at a time until smooth and creamy, then pour into a saucepan (it chills more quickly in a metal container), or into a bowl if you prefer. Whisk in the yoghurt or cream, then chill until required.

Chilled Melon and Ginger Soup

Hot sun, little crackling sounds among the wheat, increasing as the wind blew

(*Diaries,* Richard Jefferies)

Put a couple of ice cubes into a vacuum flask and pour in this soup for a refreshing cold soup for picnics or while out and about in the countryside. For al fresco dining serve in chilled bowls with a sprinkling of chopped mint and a swirl of double cream – a delicious alternative to the usual melon and ginger.

Ingredients to serve 6–8 depending on appetites

2 small Galia or 1 medium-to-large honeydew
  melon
6 pieces preserved stem ginger in syrup
225 g (8 oz) natural Greek yoghurt

1–2 tablespoons clear honey to taste
225 ml (8 fl oz) single cream
Bunch of fresh mint, washed and chopped

Method

Cut the melons in half, remove the pips and spoon the flesh into a bowl. Slice the ginger pieces and mix with the melon; stir in the yoghurt and honey. Transfer to a food processor and blend until smooth. Return the mixture to a clean bowl and stir in the cream.

Chill in the refrigerator until required. When ready to serve (if not taking on a picnic), pour the soup into soup bowls and sprinkle a little chopped mint over each serving.

Cook's note
The amount of honey will depend upon the sweetness of the melon and particular preference.

Chilled Smoked Salmon Soup

A delicious alternative to slices of smoked salmon and lemon wedges. Quail eggs are of course optional. For an informal party in the garden they can be omitted but they make a special contribution to the soup for more formal occasions.

Ingredients to serve 4–6

4 spring onions, white parts only, chopped

300 ml ($^1/_2$ pint) tomato juice

A few shakes of Tabasco to taste

3 teaspoons tomato purée

Juice of 1 lemon

250 g (9 oz) smoked salmon trimmings

3 tablespoons mayonnaise

600 ml (1 pint) fish stock

Sea salt and freshly ground black pepper

150 ml (5 fl oz) fromage frais or single cream

125 g ($4^1/_2$ oz) peeled prawns

4–6 quail eggs, hard boiled, peeled and cut in half

4–6 sprigs fresh fennel

Method

Liquidise the spring onion, tomato juice, Tabasco, tomato purée and lemon juice until smooth. Add the smoked salmon pieces and liquidise again until smooth. Pour the mixture into a large bowl and whisk in the mayonnaise, stock, sea salt, pepper, fromage frais or cream. Chill in the refrigerator.

When chilled and ready to serve, pour the soup into soup bowls and divide the prawns equally among the bowls, float 2 halves of a quail egg on top of each bowl and place a sprig of fresh fennel over the egg. Serve with slices of brown bread and butter.

Cook's note
If raw spring onion is not to your taste, sauté the chopped onions in a little hot oil for a couple of minutes and then use as described.

Courgette and Watercress Soup

Breakfast found him (William Cobbett) hungry, but he ate only a small portion of cold meat and bread, and he never touched what he called 'garden stuff'.

(*Travel in England*, Thomas Burke)

Ingredients to serve 4

55 g (2 oz) butter
1 large onion, peeled and chopped
4 large courgettes, washed, trimmed and chopped
1 bunch watercress, washed, large stalks removed
1 litre (1¾ pints) vegetable or chicken stock
150 ml (¼ pint) whole milk
1 teaspoon ground ginger
Sea salt and freshly ground black pepper to taste
80 ml (3 fl oz) double cream

Method

Melt the butter in a saucepan and add the onion, cook until soft and then add the courgettes, watercress and stock. Simmer for 10 minutes until the courgettes are soft. Remove from the heat and add the milk, ginger and season to taste. Put into a food processor and blend until smooth. Return the soup to the saucepan, stir in the cream, heat and serve.

STARTERS AND SIDE-DISHES

Fresh Peach Salad with a Blue Cheese and Walnut Dressing

According to the Reverend John A. Clark in 1840, Derby Day seemed to have the qualities of a huge picnic, a mammoth country fair, and a dangerous public riot! During the intervals between the races, the ground was filled with jugglers, gamesters, rope-dancers, fortune tellers, rows of gambling booths, splendidly hung with crimson and beautiful tapestry.

The secret of this slightly unusual salad depends upon the ripeness of the peaches (tinned peaches should not be used). The delicate fruit flavour of fresh peaches, blends surprisingly well with the blue cheese cream.

Ingredients to serve 4

4 fresh, ripe peaches
2 lettuce hearts

For the dressing

125 g (4$\frac{1}{2}$ oz) soft or hard blue-veined cheese
125 ml (4 fl oz) single cream
A little whole milk to mix
Pinch of cayenne pepper to taste
70 g (2$\frac{1}{2}$ oz) chopped walnuts

Method

To make the dressing Break the cheese into small pieces and put into a food processor. Add the cream and a small amount of milk to prevent the mixture from clogging and becoming too thick. Add the cayenne pepper to taste. Blend until smooth and creamy. Transfer to a bowl and mix in the chopped walnuts.

Peel and halve the peaches and discard the stones. Place the peaches on a plate, or in a suitable container if taking on a picnic and spoon over the dressing. When ready, serve with the lettuce heart leaves.

Goat's Cheese with Roasted Garlic

Ingredients to serve 4

1 large crown of garlic

3 sprigs fresh rosemary

2 sprigs fresh thyme

Grated rind and juice of ½ lemon

4–5 tablespoons olive oil

115 g (4 oz) soft goat's cheese

50 ml (2 fl oz) double cream or crème fraiche

½ teaspoon cayenne pepper

Slices of toasted French bread or farmhouse
  crusty bread

Salt and ground black pepper to taste

Several leaves of fresh chicory

Method

Pre-heat the oven to 400ºC/200ºF/gas mark 6. Slice the top off the garlic, just enough to allow the oil to be absorbed, then put it into an ovenproof dish; season to taste with salt and pepper; add the herbs, sprinkle over lemon rind and juice, and pour in the olive oil. Cover with kitchen foil and cook in the pre-heated oven for 10 minutes. After that time, baste with the hot oil in the dish. Lower the temperature to 170ºC/325ºF/gas mark 3 and cook for a further 35–40 minutes. (Garlic cooks more evenly when roasted slowly at a low temperature.) When ready, the garlic should be soft and squashy. Squeeze the pulp from the roasted garlic and discard the papery skin.

   Put the goat's cheese into a mixing bowl and squash with a fork. Mix in the roasted garlic pulp then blend with the cream or crème fraiche to a smooth paste. Stir in the cayenne pepper, pile onto the slices of toasted bread, and serve with chicory leaves and the roasted garlic. Pour a little of the cooking juices over each portion.

Cook's note
Roast garlic can be stored in its pulped state in a small jar and kept in the refrigerator until required.

Ham and Tarragon Mousse

'That's a monstrous fine ham,' observed he; 'why doesn't somebody cut it?' 'Let me help you to some, sir' replied Mr Springwheat, seizing the buck-handled knife and fork, and diving deep into the rich red meat with the knife.

(Mr Sponge's Sporting Tour, R. S. Surtees)

The basis of this mousse is the béchamel sauce – a 'foundation' sauce used for many recipes, and a well made sauce makes all the difference to the flavour of a dish. For picnics or lunch outside the mousse can be spooned straight from the bowl, or turned out and decorated for a more formal occasion.

Ingredients to serve 4–6

425 g (15 oz) good flavoured cooked ham

225 ml (8 fl oz) béchamel sauce

1 teaspoon fresh tarragon, finely chopped

Sea salt and freshly ground black pepper to taste

3 tablespoons made mayonnaise

150 ml ($^1/_4$ pint) whipping cream

For the béchamel sauce

225 ml (8 fl oz) whole milk

1 shallot, peeled and finely sliced

$^1/_2$ carrot, peeled and cut into 'matchsticks'

1 small stick celery, washed, cut into 'matchsticks'

4 black pepper corns, crushed

1 small bay leaf

55 g (2 oz) unsalted butter

55 g (2 oz) plain flour

Sea salt and freshly ground black pepper to taste

3 sheets leaf gelatine, soaked in a little cold water

To garnish

sliced cucumber, cherry tomatoes, fresh tarragon leaves

Method

To make the béchamel sauce Put all ingredients into the saucepan except for the butter and flour. Bring to the boil and simmer for a couple of minutes until the vegetables are soft. Remove from the heat, cover and leave to infuse for around 15 minutes. After that time, strain through a sieve into a jug, press the vegetables with the back of a spoon to squeeze out all the flavour and then discard the contents of the sieve.

Melt the butter in a small saucepan and, using a wooden spoon, mix in the flour stirring all the time until the mixture is smooth. Cook over a gentle heat for 2–3 minutes, stirring all the time until the mixture begins to bubble. Remove from the heat and gradually pour in the infused milk, stirring after each addition to prevent lumps from forming. Return to the heat and bring the sauce to the boil stirring continuously. Once the sauce has thickened, season to taste and cook for a further 2 minutes. Remove from the heat, drop in the soaked gelatine leaves and beat into the sauce until well blended. Pour the sauce into a bowl and leave to cool. The béchamel must be completely cold before adding the ham, mayonnaise and cream.

Chop the ham very finely (this can be done in a food processor). Fold the chopped ham, tarragon and mayonnaise into the cold béchamel sauce. Lightly whip the cream and gently fold into the mousse mixture. Transfer to a serving bowl, cover and put into the refrigerator to set. When set and ready to serve, decorate the top of the mousse with thin slices of cucumber, halved cherry tomatoes and fresh tarragon leaves.

Cook's note
For a stronger flavour, add a couple of teaspoons of Dijon mustard when adding the mayonnaise, and smoked ham can be used instead of usual ham.

Jellied Tomato and Basil Consommé

When searching through some old cookery books, we came across a version of this recipe and it gave us an idea of what to do with a glut of tomatoes. Tested and adapted, a fairly ordinary 'tomato mould' (its original name) became transformed into a refreshing and unusual starter. The centre of the ring mould can be filled with a variety of your favourite ingredients – we use chopped spring onions and peas, cherry tomatoes, watercress, prawns in mayonnaise or for special occasions peppered smoked salmon rolls sprinkled with lemon vinaigrette dressing.

Made in advance, this is an ideal dish for entertaining. All you have to do when it is required is to remove the consommé from the refrigerator, pile your chosen filling in the middle and take it to the table.

Ingredients to serve 8

4 sheets gelatine

900 g (2 lb) ripe tomatoes, skinned and chopped

2 bay leaves

300 ml ($^{1}/_{2}$ pint) white wine

4 tablespoons white wine vinegar

1 level tablespoon tomato purée

1 crushed clove garlic

Grated rind and juice of a lemon

1 tablespoon Demerara sugar

Sea salt and freshly ground black pepper

6 large basil leaves

Method

Lay the sheets of gelatine in a bowl of cold water to become 'floppy'.

In a large saucepan put the tomatoes, bay leaves, wine, wine vinegar, tomato purée, garlic, lemon rind and juice, sugar, salt and pepper to taste. Simmer for 10–15 minutes until the sugar has dissolved then turn off the heat.

Drain the water from the gelatine and drop the sheets into the hot tomato mixture, blend well in and then allow ingredients to infuse for 20 minutes. After that time, strain the liquid into a bowl through a fine sieve. Lightly oil a ring mould and pour in the strained tomato mixture. Chop the basil and sprinkle into the consommé; put into the refrigerator to set overnight. When ready to serve, turn out onto a dish and pile your chosen filling into the centre and serve with brown bread and butter.

Fresh Pear and Stilton Flan

A husband and wife were at a race meeting. 'Pink Nightie' had just come in, in second place; the man knew that his wife had backed it. 'Did you back it both ways?' enquired the husband anxiously. 'No dear, how foolish of me,' she said, 'I didn't realise they were coming back.'

(Sporting and Dramatic Yarns, R. J. B. Stellar)

This flan would make a good 'peace offering' and will appease any sportsman's appetite. It can be taken on a picnic, served as a starter or main course for lunch or supper, and is as delicious cold as it is hot.

Ingredients to serve 4

225 g (8 oz) short crust pastry

55 g (2 oz) unsalted butter

1 large onion, peeled and thinly sliced

2 ripe pears

150 ml (¼ pint) single cream

2 large eggs

1 tablespoon freshly chopped parsley

85 g (3 oz) Stilton cheese, rind removed

Sea salt and black pepper to taste

Method

Pre-heat the oven to 190ºC/375ºF/gas mark 5. Line a flan ring with the rolled-out pastry and put in the oven to cook 'blind' (empty). Take care not to over-brown.

Melt the butter in a saucepan, put in the onion and cook until soft. Remove from the heat, allow to cool, and then line the bottom of the pastry case. Peel, core and slice the pears and lay them evenly over the onion; season well to taste. Put the cream, eggs, parsley and Stilton into a liquidiser and blend until smooth and creamy. Pour the sauce over the pears and onion. Cook in the pre-heated oven for 25–30 minutes until the mixture has set and is golden brown.

Mango Vinaigrette Salad

A colourful salad, a good accompaniment to smoked meats such as chicken, venison, duck, ham and smoked fish.

Ingredients to serve 4

For the vinaigrette

1 small, very ripe mango

3 tablespoons red wine or raspberry vinegar

Juice of $^1/_2$ lemon

1 teasooon French mustard

2 tablespoons clear honey

Sea salt and freshly ground black pepper

150 ml ($^1/_4$ pint) sunflower oil

1 tablespoon finely chopped parsley

For the salad

2 bunches rocket

2 bunches watercress

70 g ($2^1/_2$ oz) spinach

2 Little Gem lettuces

1 orange, peeled, pith removed and
  segmented

1 tablespoon slivered almonds

1 ripe mango

Method

To make the vinaigrette Peel the mango and slice the flesh from the stone, put the flesh into a food processor or blender and add the vinegar, lemon juice, mustard, honey, salt and pepper to taste. Blend until smooth. Still blending, gradually pour in the oil until the mixture thickens slightly and has a smooth consistency. Pour into a jug and stir in the chopped parsley. Check the seasonings for taste.

Wash the rocket, watercress and spinach, dry well and put into a large salad or mixing bowl. Wash and chop the lettuces and add these to the bowl. Toss in the orange segments and almonds. Peel the mango and slice the flesh from the stone; put the flesh into the bowl. Drizzle over some of the mango dressing and toss the salad well together.

Potato, Mint and Gherkin Loaf

Clock golf, bowls and croquet – three games for which no particular freedom of dress is required – are good pastimes for garden parties. Tennis can only be included in the programme if you have announced it on your invitation cards…otherwise shoes and rackets will be wanting. To say nothing of the unsuitability of the gala clothes your visitors will probably have chosen to wear.

(*The Pleasure of Your Company,* June and Doris Langley Moore)

An excellent out-of-doors dish; the perfect complement to any buffet table. Easily transportable, made in advance and versatile as an accompaniment or as a main dish, if you add a 1–2 tablespoons of chopped ham or chicken to the ingredients.

Ingredients to serve 6–8

450 g (1 lb) potatoes peeled and cut into small pieces

300 ml ($^1/_2$ pint) whole milk

2 teaspoons cornflour mixed to a paste with 100 ml ($3^1/_2$ fl oz) water

4 spring onions, trimmed and chopped

3 pickled gherkins, chopped

2 tablespoons fresh mint, chopped

3 tablespoons mayonnaise

3 tablespoons fromage frais

Sea salt and freshly ground black pepper to taste

Cayenne pepper to taste

Lettuce leaves, and chopped mint to garnish

Method

Put the potato into a saucepan and pour in the milk. Cook the potatoes until almost tender. Pour in the slackened cornflour and continue to cook briefly, until the flour is cooked and the mixture has thickened. Transfer to a mixing bowl and mix in the spring onion, gherkin and mint. Blend well together. Allow to cool a little and then fold in the mayonnaise and fromage frais, blending well. Season to taste with the salt and peppers and blend again until all ingredients are thoroughly blended together.

Line a 450 g (1 lb) loaf tin with greaseproof paper and spoon in the potato mixture. Set in the refrigerator for 2–3 hours or overnight. Turn out onto a bed of lettuce leaves and sprinkle over chopped mint and a few borage or chive flowers if available.

FISH

Crab Tartlet

All things that love the sun are out of doors;
The sky rejoices in the morning's birth;
The grass is bright with rain-drops-on the moors.

(*Resolution and Independence,* William Wordsworth)

These tartlets have a fresh, delicate flavour and mustn't be over-heated at the final stage of baking. If you're feeling extravagant, substitute fresh lobster.

250 g (9 oz) short crust pastry

2 teaspoons chives, freshly chopped

1 tablespoon tarragon, freshly chopped

125 ml (4 fl oz) natural Greek yoghurt

225 ml (8 fl oz) double cream

Grated rind and juice of 1 small lemon

2 teaspoons sugar

Sea salt and freshly ground black pepper

A good shake of cayenne pepper

1 large dressed crab

Method

Pre-heat the oven to 190ºC/375ºF/gas mark 5. Roll out the pastry and cut out 4 equal-sized circles. Press them into a patty tin and bake 'blind' until a pale golden colour.

Put all the other ingredients except for the crab meat into a food processor and blend until smooth. Transfer to a basin.

Remove the crab meat from the shell and put the meat into a basin. Fold 4 level tablespoons of the blended cream and herb mixture into the crab meat and blend well in. Put the baked tartlet cases onto a baking tray and divide the crab mixture evenly between them. Spoon the remaining herb cream over each one. Bake the tartlets in the pre-heated oven for 10–15 minutes until heated through. Serve immediately.

Double Salmon Mousse

This attractive dish can be served as a starter, light lunch, taken on a picnic or will look resplendent on the buffet table.

Ingredients to serve 4 as a starter

4 slices smoked salmon

170 g (6 oz) salmon fillets

150 ml ($^1/_4$ pint) water for poaching

25 g (1 oz) unsalted butter

25 g (1 oz) plain flour

Juice of $^1/_2$ lemon

Cayenne pepper to taste

Pinch of sea salt

100 ml ($3^1/_2$ fl oz) double cream

4 slices wholemeal bread

Method

Line the bottom of 4 ramekins with a circle of greaseproof paper and then line sides and bottoms of the ramekins with strips of smoked salmon.

Poach the salmon fillets in the water until tender, drain and reserve the poaching liquid for the sauce.

Melt the butter in a saucepan, add the flour and stir and cook for 2 minutes and then remove from the heat and pour in the poaching liquid. Stir until well blended.

Pound the cooked salmon and add to the sauce; blend in the lemon juice, cayenne pepper and the sea salt. Allow to cool.

Lightly whip the cream and fold into the cooled sauce. Pour the sauce mixture into the prepared ramekins.

Cut four circles of wholemeal bread the size of the ramekin, butter one side and place on top of the mousse; when the mousse is turned out it will be sitting on a bread base.

When required: take a sharp knife and run the blade around the edge of the mousse to loosen, turn out onto a dish, removing the circle of greaseproof paper.

Smoked Salmon Cheesecake

This elegant cheesecake is a real party piece: pleasing to the eye and taste buds. Oak-smoked salmon has a stronger flavour and is best for this recipe, but a well-flavoured smoked salmon will suffice.

Cut as a cake, this cheesecake will go a long way, and is excellent for summer parties and sporting picnics.

Ingredients to serve 14

For the base

140 g (5 oz) wholemeal cream crackers

1 packet Ritz crackers

115 g (4 oz) butter, melted

For the topping

450 g (1 lb) smoked salmon, skin removed

400 g (14 oz) light cream cheese

400 ml (13 fl oz) natural Greek yoghurt

Finely grated rind and juice of 1 lemon

125 ml (4 fl oz) milk

3 sheets leaf gelatine, soaked in a little cold water

Small bunch chives, finely chopped

Freshly ground black or white pepper to taste

Lemon and cucumber to garnish

Method

For the base Crush the savoury biscuits in a food processor, pour in the melted butter and whiz briefly to blend. Tip out into a 25 cm (10 inch) cake tin and press the crushed biscuit firmly onto the base, easing it approximately 2.5 cm (1¼ inches) up the side of the tin. Refrigerate until set.

For the topping Cut the smoked salmon into pieces, and put into a food processor with the cream cheese, yoghurt, lemon rind and juice. Blend until smooth. Heat the milk. When hot, remove from the heat and drop in the soaked gelatine, blend well until dissolved. Pour into the salmon mixture in the food processor, add the chopped chives, season to taste with the pepper and blend again until all ingredients are well incorporated. Pour onto the set biscuit base and refrigerate again for 2–3 hours until required. Remove the cheesecake from the tin, garnish with slices of fresh lemon and cucumber.

Salmon Slippers with Date Mayonnaise

The chaplain's errand was to inform us that Mr Thornhill had provided music and refreshments; and intended that night giving the young ladies a ball by moonlight, on the grass plot before our very door.

(The Vicar of Wakefield, Oliver Goldsmith)

A sixteenth century dish deriving its name from the pastry case that encloses the salmon (something inside, as a foot in a slipper). A perfect dish for a Midsummer's eve party, and if you can schedule your party to coincide with the full moon, so much the better.

Ingredients to serve 4

375 g (13 oz) puff pastry
4 skinless fillets of salmon
4 fresh stoneless dates, finely chopped
2 pieces preserved stem ginger, syrup washed off with cold water
1 tablespoon tarragon, chopped
1 tablespoon blanched almonds, chopped
Grated rind and juice of $1/2$ lemon
Sea salt and freshly ground black pepper to taste

For the date mayonnaise

4 stoneless dates soaked in a little water for $1/2$ hour
$1/2$ clove garlic, crushed
2 tablespoons lemon oil
4 tablespoons light olive oil
4 teaspoons lemon juice
1 tablespoon double cream

Method

Roll out the pastry and cut into 4 even-sized rectangles slightly larger than the salmon fillets. Lay a fillet of salmon in the centre of each pastry rectangle and top each fillet with a layer each of chopped dates, almonds, ginger and tarragon. Sprinkle over the lemon zest and juice, season to taste. Bring the sides of the pastry up over the fish leaving a 2.5 cm (1 inch) gap at the top forming the 'slipper'. Crimp the edges lightly between thumb and forefinger. Chill in the refrigerator at least $^1/_2$ hour before baking.

When ready, bake in a hot oven 200ºC/400ºF/gas mark 6 for 15 minutes, until the pastry is cooked and golden. Cooking time may vary slightly depending on size and thickness of the salmon fillets.

To make the date mayonnaise Remove the soaked prunes from the water and put into a pestle and mortar; add the crushed garlic and mix together until smooth. Drizzle in the oil a little at a time blending well between each addition. Blend together until the mixture thickens and becomes a creamy texture. Blend in the lemon juice and cream then transfer to a bowl and serve with the baked salmon slippers.

Sole Fillets with Fresh Orange Mayonnaise

Come when the leaf comes, angle with me,
Come when the bee hums, crossing the lea;
Come with the wild flowers
Come with the mild showers,
Come when the singing bird calleth for thee.

(*An Angler's Invitation,* Thomas Tod Stoddart)

Served cold, this dish is great for lunch in the garden or for a picnic on the bowling or cricket green. It also doubles as an easy main course for a summer dinner party.

Ingredients to serve 4

4 large lemon sole fillets, skin removed
2 tablespoons white wine
Juice of 1 small lemon
40 g (1¹/₂ oz) butter
Sprig of fresh tarragon
Sea salt and white pepper to taste
10–12 Little Gem lettuce leaves, washed
4 oranges, peeled and segmented
1 tablespoon parsley, chopped

For the orange mayonnaise

150 ml (¹/₄ pint) made mayonnaise
Grated rind of 1 orange
2 teaspoons white wine vinegar
1 teaspoon caster sugar

Method

Pre-heat the oven to 180ºC/350ºF/gas mark 4. Line an ovenproof dish with foil, roll up the sole fillets and lay them on the foil in the dish. Pour in the wine and lemon juice, dot the fish with the butter, lay the sprig of tarragon on top, season to taste and fold the foil over the fish to form a tight parcel. Cook in the pre-heated oven for 20 minutes. When cooked, remove the from the oven, open up the parcel and allow to cool.

To make the orange mayonnaise Put the made mayonnaise into a bowl, add the orange rind, wine vinegar and sugar. Blend the ingredients well together then set aside.

Lay the lettuce leaves on a serving dish and when the fillets are cool, remove the fish only from the foil and lay the fillets on the bed of lettuce. Coat each one with the prepared orange mayonnaise and arrange the orange segments around the fish. Sprinkle over chopped parsley.

Cook's note
The juice from the orange is not used in the mayonnaise as it would make the consistency too runny and would overpower the delicate flavour of the sole fillet. The grated rind is sufficient. However, the juice can be reserved for salad dressing.

MAIN COURSES

Chicken and Tarragon Terrine

Ingredients to serve 4

55g (2 oz) butter

2 shallots, thinly sliced

1 small carrot cut into 'matchsticks'

2 tablespoons fresh tarragon, chopped

4 chicken breasts

4 tablespoons white wine

1 teaspoon powdered chicken stock

150 ml (¹/₄ pint) hot water

Sea salt and freshly ground black pepper to taste

3 sheets leaf gelatine, soaked in cold water

150 ml (¹/₄ pint) crème fraîche or double cream

2–3 sprigs tarragon for garnishing

Method

Pre-heat the oven to 180ºC/350ºF/gas mark 4. Melt the butter in a frying pan and lightly sauté the shallot and carrot until just soft. Lay the sautéed onion and carrot on the bottom of an ovenproof dish, sprinkle over 1 tablespoon of chopped tarragon, and then place the chicken breasts on top. Pour over the white wine. Mix the stock powder with the hot water, pour over the chicken and season to taste. Cook in the pre-heated oven for 20–25 minutes until the chicken is tender.

Remove the dish from the oven and take out the chicken. Strain the juices, into a bowl and whisk in the soaked gelatine leaves. Discard the vegetables. Pour the liquid into a food processor, add the remaining tablespoon of chopped tarragon, the crème fraîche or cream and blend until smooth.

When the cooked chicken breasts have cooled, finely chop into small pieces. (You can mince, if preferred.) Add the liquidised sauce and blend well in. Check the seasonings and pile the mixture into an earthenware or other suitable container. Set in the refrigerator until firm. When required, turn the terrine out onto a serving plate and decorate with slices of cucumber and a few sprigs of tarragon.

Curried Fruity Chicken

Goodwood is perfect when the weather is fine, a real racing picnic.

(*Chit-Chat,* Lady Augusta Fane)

A lovely fresh dish, perfect for a racing picnic, especially if the weather is warm and sunny. The dish does have to be made on the day because of the fruit, and ripe well-flavoured peaches are essential to the flavour. However it is such an easy recipe to prepare and should only take approximately 15–20 minutes.

Curried fruity chicken is also suitable for a summer dinner party arranged on a pretty serving dish in a circle of crisp lettuce leaves and sprinkled with chopped parsley.

Ingredients to serve 4–6

6 ready-cooked, skinless, boneless chicken
  breasts
150 ml (5 fl oz) whipping cream
4 teaspoons curry paste
125 ml (4 fl oz) fromage frais
2 large bananas

170 g (6 oz) seedless grapes, cut in half
2 eating apples, peeled, cored and sliced
2 ripe peaches, skinned, stones removed
Sea salt and freshly ground black pepper
Crisp lettuce leaves for serving

Method

Cut the chicken into bite-sized pieces and set aside. Pour the cream into a large bowl, add the curry paste and whisk together until the cream just holds its shape (it should be a 'coating' consistency) and then fold in the fromage frais. Peel the banana, cut the flesh into chunks and fold into the curried cream. Fold in the grapes and apple slices. Slice the peach and fold into the cream and fruit. Lastly, fold in the chicken pieces and season to taste. Put into a suitable container and refrigerate until required. Serve with boiled rice with flaked almonds and a green salad.

Lime and Honey Marinated Chicken

'And now you all know each other, let's be comfortable and happy, and see what's going forward; that's what I say…Undo the hamper, Joe.'

(*The Pickwick Papers,* Charles Dickens)

Marinating tenderises meat and imparts flavour, ideal for a barbecue picnic or grilling at home. Lamb or pork chops can also be done in the same way as chicken.

Ingredients to serve 4

8 chicken drumsticks or 4 chicken breasts

For the marinade
1 clove garlic, crushed
Pinch of sea salt and freshly ground black pepper
Juice and grated rind of 1 lime
2 tablespoons clear honey
2 tablespoons vegetable oil
2 teaspoons thyme leaves, freshly chopped
2 teaspoons white wine vinegar

Method

Put all the marinade ingredients into a large bowl, stir until the ingredients are blended together and put in the chicken making sure all the meat is well covered.

Marinade for 4–6 hours or overnight in a cool place, turning from time to time.

When ready to eat, remove the chicken from the marinade, place on the barbecue or on a grill pan, brush over a little marinade and over or under a moderate heat, barbecue or grill until the meat is tender. The honey should be just caramelised to give the meat a light crunchy coating.

Poulet Chantilly *(A Chilled Chicken Salad)*

Leathery breeches, spreading stables,
Shining saddles left behind –
To the down the string of horses
Moving out of sight and mind.

(*Upper Lambourne*, John Betjeman)

Chantilly is French for lace, which describes this delicious dish perfectly – your time spent in preparation will be well rewarded when your guests enjoy the delicate flavour and elegant presentation. It is the ideal party dish for any elegant outdoor occasion being easily transportable. The rice and vegetables are best cooked the day before, and then all you have to do on the day is cut up the chicken and fold into the Chantilly mayonnaise.

Ingredients to serve 4–6

2 red peppers

150 ml (¹/₄ pint) white wine (White Burgundy)

Juice of ¹/₂ lemon

150 ml (¹/₄ pint) olive oil

300 ml (¹/₂ pint) chicken or vegetable stock

115 g (4 oz) button mushrooms, wiped and cut into quarters

8 shallots, peeled, cut in half

1 skinned tomato, quartered

1 bay leaf

Sea salt and freshly ground black pepper to taste

40 g (1¹/₂ oz) unsalted butter

225 g (8 oz) rice

1 good-sized ready-cooked chicken, skin removed

300 ml (¹/₂ pint) double cream or crème fraîche

300 ml (¹/₂ pint) made mayonnaise

2 Little Gem lettuces, washed

1 hard boiled egg

Method

Cut the peppers in half and remove the pith and seeds. Cut into strips and put in a pan of cold water, and boil for 5 minutes. Remove the peppers, drain and put to one side.

Into a large saucepan put wine, oil, lemon juice, stock, mushrooms, onions, tomato and the bay leaf. Season to taste. Boil all together for 7–10 minutes until the shallots are soft. Strain the liquid into a measuring jug and make up with extra stock to 600 ml (1 pint).

Melt the butter in a large saucepan and add the rice, stirring over a low heat until the rice is opaque. Remove from the heat and put in the liquid, onions, mushrooms and tomato discarding the bay leaf. Check the seasonings and transfer the rice and vegetables to an ovenproof dish; cover with greaseproof paper and a lid, and cook in a moderate oven 190ºC/375ºF/gas mark 5 for 25–30 minutes until the rice is tender. When ready, remove from the oven and spread on a large plate to cool.

Remove the cooked chicken from the bone and cut into bite sized chunks. Whip the cream or crème fraîche until fairly stiff and fold into the mayonnaise. Then fold in the chicken pieces.

Heap the cooled rice onto a large serving dish and make a well in the centre. Arrange the lettuce leaves around the inside edge of the well. Pile the chicken and mayonnaise into the well. Chop the egg into small pieces and with the strips of red pepper, scatter over the top of the rice.

Cook's note
For quickness, ready-cooked, skinless chicken breasts can be used instead of a whole chicken if you prefer – one chicken breast for each person. If the whole dish is prepared in advance and kept in the refrigerator, the flavour improves as it chills.

Pigeon Pie *(Epsom Grandstand recipe)*

22nd May 1867. The day dawned grey and bitterly cold. As the day wore on, biting winds, sleet and finally flurries of snow swept across Epsom Downs. The huge crowds, which normally flocked to the course from London, were reduced to a trickle.

(The Pocket Venus, Henry Blyth)

The Times, in a subsequent report of the scene, referred to the inclement weather which froze the general current gaiety of the holiday-makers. There was a forest of umbrellas on the course and in the stands, and the race goers slapped their hands for warmth as they watched the horses parading in the paddock.

The original recipe called for uncooked, whole pigeons but we have adapted the recipe to a more convenient method. Pigeon breasts can be bought from most good game butchers and supermarkets.

Ingredients to serve 4–6

4–6 pigeon beasts, thinly sliced
750 g (1 lb 10 oz) rump steak, cut into pieces
1 tablespoon plain flour sifted with a teaspoon of salt
4–6 tablespoons olive oil for frying
8 rashers rindless streaky bacon, cut into small pieces
1 onion, peeled and chopped
600 ml (1 pint) beef stock
125 ml (4 fl oz) tawny port
1 large sprig of thyme
Sea salt and ground black pepper
4–6 hard-boiled eggs, shells removed
450 g (1 lb) puff pastry
1 beaten egg for glazing

Method

Toss the pigeon slices and steak pieces in the seasoned flour. Heat the oil in a large heavy-based saucepan and fry the bacon until the fat begins to run. Remove from the pan and set aside. Put the onion in the pan and cook until soft, remove and put with the bacon. Add a little more oil if necessary and fry the steak a few pieces at a time. When all the steak is nicely browned, put with the bacon and onion. Put the pigeon slices into the pan and fry just enough to seal in the juices. Return the steak, onion and bacon to the pan, pour in the stock, add the port and sprig of thyme; season to taste, cover the pan and simmer for 1-2 hours until the meat is tender and the liquid reduced.

When ready, remove from the heat and allow to cool completely.

Pre-heat the oven to 200ºC/400ºF/gas mark 6. Place a pie funnel in the centre of the dish. Roll out the pastry and cut out a long, thin strip, lay it around the edge of the dish and dampen with a little water or milk. Tip the contents of the saucepan into the pie dish including the cooking juices. Press the hard-boiled eggs into the meat, cover over with the rolled-out pastry to form a lid, sealing the edges well. Brush the pastry with the beaten egg and bake in the pre-heated oven for 20 minutes to brown the pastry.

Cook's note
If the pie has to wait, lower the oven temperature to 150ºC/300ºF/gas mark 2. Don't over boil the eggs – if they are too hard, they will become rubbery when cooking in the pie.

Roast Grouse with Apple and Sage Sauce

Ingredients to serve 2–3

2 oven-ready young grouse, cleaned and
  trussed
1 large eating apple, peeled, cored and cut
  into pieces
2 walnut-sized pieces butter
6 rashers smoked, streaky bacon
4 tablespoons Calvados

For the sauce

2 cooking apples, peeled, cored and sliced
150 ml (¼ pint) apple juice
2 fresh sage leaves, washed and finely
  chopped

Method

For the grouse

Pre-heat the oven to 200°C/400°F/gas mark 6. Place a knob of butter and half the apple pieces inside each bird. Envelope each bird with the slices of bacon and cover each bird with a sheet of kitchen foil. Pour a little water into a roasting pan and put in the bacon-covered grouse. Roast in the pre-heated oven for 20–30 minutes depending on the size of birds. Remove the foil and cook for a further 10 minutes to brown.

To make the sauce Put the sliced apples into a saucepan, pour in the apple juice and cook until the apple is soft. Stir in the chopped sage leaves and cook for a further 2–3 minutes. Set aside.

When the grouse are cooked, remove from the oven and put them onto a dish and keep warm. Pour the Calvados into the roasting pan and scrape round to deglaze, gathering all the meat juices. Pour the juices into the apple sauce mixture and then transfer the sauce to a food processor and blend until smooth. If the sauce is too thick for your liking, slacken with a little more apple juice or water. Carve the grouse and serve with the sauce, poured over or separately.

Steak Tartare

This is former National Hunt jockey Terry Biddlecombe's variation of this classic dish. It is very simple to prepare and requires no cooking, but because of this, the fillet steak must be of the best quality. Terry recommends that it should be followed by three large glasses of port, vintage or non-vintage, depending upon who's paying.

Ingredients to serve 2

300 g (10$^{1}/_{2}$ oz) fillet steak, finely chopped

1 small onion, peeled and grated

2 cloves garlic, crushed

$^{1}/_{2}$ teaspoon capers

2 teaspoons gherkins, finely chopped

Dash Tabasco sauce

2 teaspoons Worcestershire sauce

Salt and black pepper to taste

1 egg yolk, beaten

2 tablespoons brandy

Method

Put all the ingredients into a bowl and mix thoroughly together. Divide between two plates, shape into a circle and serve with a mixed green salad and French dressing.

Steak Tartare – Cooked Method

Ingredients to serve 2

2 fillet steaks

2 shallots, finely chopped

1–2 tablespoons olive oil

1 clove garlic, crushed

$^1/_2$ teaspoon capers

2 teaspoons gherkin, finely chopped

Dash of Tabasco

2 teaspoons Worcestershire sauce

2 tablespoons brandy

100 ml (3$^1/_2$ fl oz) beef stock

Method

Heat the oil in a frying pan and cook the steaks to your liking, remove from the pan and keep warm. Add a little more olive oil to the pan if necessary and cook the shallots and garlic for 1 minute. Stir in the capers, gherkins, Tabasco, Worcestershire sauce, brandy and beef stock, and simmer to reduce the liquid by half. Season to taste and serve with the cooked steak.

Tenderloin of Pork with Lemon and Mushroom Sauce

At the summit of the Pike there was not a breath of air to stir even the papers, which we spread out containing our food. There we ate our dinner in summer warmth; and the stillness seemed to be not of this world.

(An Excursion up Scawfell Pike, Dorothy Wordsworth)

The flavour of this dish is in the creamy sauce and is well worth taking time to prepare. You may need to give your guests a spoon for any sauce left on the plate – it is just too good to waste.

Ingredients to serve 4–6

2 pork tenderloins

1 tablespoon plain flour sifted with a level teaspoon sea salt

For the sauce

115 g (4 oz) unsalted butter

170 g (6 oz) field mushrooms, wiped and thinly sliced

70 g (2$^{1}/_{2}$ oz) plain flour

600 ml (1 pint) whole milk

1 teaspoon fresh parsley, chopped

1 teaspoon chives, chopped

Finely grated rind and juice of 2 lemons

1 level tablespoon caster sugar

Sea salt and freshly ground black pepper

150 ml ($^{1}/_{4}$ pint) vegetable oil

Chopped fresh parsley to garnish

Method

Cut the pork tenderloins into pieces approximately 2.5 cm (1 inch) thick, removing any white skin. Place the pieces of pork, cut side down between two pieces of strong cling film and, with a rolling pin, flatten the pieces into 'medallions'. Remove the cling film and dust the pork with the seasoned flour, put to one side.

To make the sauce Melt half the butter in a saucepan, add the mushroom slices and cook over a low heat stirring all the time, until they change colour and the juices begin to run. Remove the mushrooms and set aside. Put the remaining butter into the pan and when melted, add the flour and cook for 2 minutes. Pour in the milk a little at a time beating well. Add the herbs, lemon rind and juice, sugar and the cooked mushrooms. Season to taste and simmer gently while the pork is cooking.

Put the oil into a frying pan, add the pork pieces a few at a time and sauté for 2–3 minutes on each side, removing the pork as you go and keeping the pieces warm. When all the pork pieces have been sautéed, lay them on a warm serving dish and pour over the mushroom sauce. Sprinkle with chopped parsley and serve.

Serving suggestion Creamed potatoes, green beans and petit pois.

Cook's note
Don't be tempted to remove the sugar - adding the sugar prevents the sauce from curdling. However, if preferred, a light, flavoured honey will do the same thing.

Tomato, Anchovy and Olive Crumble

Ingredients to serve 4–6

10 black olives

450 g (1 lb) tomatoes, skinned and chopped

1 clove garlic, crushed

1 level tablespoon tomato purée

$^{1}/_{2}$ teaspoon fruit sugar (optional)

1 tin anchovies in olive oil, drained

4 tablespoons semi-skimmed milk

5 rounded tablespoons wholemeal breadcrumbs

4–5 tablespoons olive oil

Ground black pepper

Method

Pre-heat the oven to 180ºC/350ºF/gas mark 4. Put the prepared tomatoes into a large mixing bowl; add the olives, crushed garlic, fruit sugar if used and tomato purée. Season to taste with the pepper and mix all ingredients well together.

Soak the drained anchovies in the milk, stirring well to remove saltiness. Remove anchovies from the milk, pat dry with kitchen paper. Chop the anchovies into pieces and then stir them well into the tomato mixture. Pile the mixture into an ovenproof dish.

Mix the breadcrumbs with the olive oil until thoroughly coated, then spread evenly over the mixture. Cook in the pre-heated oven for 20–25 minutes, until hot, brown and crunchy.

Serving suggestion Roast asparagus and green leaf salad.

PUDDINGS

Chocolate Cheesecake

Table set with linen cloth,
Milk jug filled with creamy froth,
Cucumber sandwiches, bread, home baked
Chocolate cheesecake and a ginger cake.
Good thinks to eat, on a July Sunday

(*A July Sunday,* Nikki Rowan-Kedge)

Ingredients to serve 6

170 g (6 oz) digestive biscuits,
  crushed
100 g (3¹/₂ oz) butter, melted
225 g (8 oz) plain chocolate

225 g (8 oz) curd cheese
85 g (3 oz) caster sugar
150 ml (¹/₄ pint) natural yoghurt
80 ml (3 fl oz) double cream

Method

Mix the biscuit crumbs and melted butter together, press onto the base of 23-cm (9-inch) loose-bottomed cake tin. Break the chocolate into squares reserving 3 squares for decoration. Melt the remaining chocolate over hot water: this can be done in a double saucepan or in a basin standing over a saucepan of hot water. Put the curd cheese, sugar, melted chocolate and yoghurt into a food processor and blend until smooth.

Whip the cream, transfer the chocolate mixture from the blender into the cream and fold in well. Pile the cheesecake mixture into the cake tin, spreading it evenly over the crushed biscuit base. Put in the refrigerator to set until firm. When ready to serve, loosen the sides of the cake tin, run a thin knife between the base of the tin and the biscuit base and slide onto a flat plate. Grate the reserved chocolate squares and sprinkle over the outer edge of the cheesecake.

Elderflower and Rose Petal Sorbet

Good scented red roses are essential for this recipe. They give a strong scent and a beautiful pink colour to the sorbet. Made the day before, it's the perfect pudding to end a summer garden party.

Ingredients to serve 6

450 ml ($^3/_4$ pint) water

300 g ($10^1/_2$ oz) caster sugar

Grated rind and juice of 2 lemons

1 litre freshly picked elderflowers, stalks removed

1 litre freshly picked rose petals

4 tablespoons triple-strength rose water

Rose petals and elderflowers to decorate

Method

Put the water, sugar, lemon rind and juice into a saucepan. Heat gently until the sugar has dissolved and then remove from the heat. Steep the elderflowers and rose petals in the sugar syrup until the syrup is cold. Strain through muslin into a bowl then discard the elderflowers and rose petals. Stir in the rose water, pour into a suitable container and freeze.

When required, remove from the freezer about 20 minutes before serving. Use a spoon to scrape the sorbet from the container into a light 'snow' and pile into serving glasses. Decorate with fresh rose petals and a small sprig of elderflowers.

Fresh Lime Parfait

Ingredients to serve 4

Grated rind of 3 limes and juice of 4

125 g (4 oz) caster sugar

Pinch of salt

3 egg yolks

150 ml (¼ pint) whipping cream

Method

Put the lime juice and grated rind into the top of a double boiler or saucepan; add the sugar and the pinch of salt. Stand the pan over a saucepan of hot water and heat until the sugar has dissolved.

Beat the egg yolks until thick and lemon-coloured and add to the lime and sugar syrup; beat constantly over hot water until the mixture thickens. Remove from the heat and stand the double boiler or saucepan in cold water to cool quickly, whisking frequently to ensure the mixture is as light as possible.

Whip the cream until light but not too stiff and fold into the parfait mixture. Put into a suitable container and freeze until required.

When required, remove from the freezer and put into the refrigerator for 15–20 minutes before using.

Cook's note
The parfait is delicious served with rice pudding or can be served accompanied with almond or ginger biscuits.

Fruity Almond Cream

The Victorians were the first to establish the open-air party on firm foundations. They loved picnics, boating excursions, walking and skating, and they would have been exceedingly bored with the monotonous sort of life that was called a round of pleasure by their grandmothers.

(*The Pleasure of Your Company,* June and Doris Langley Moore)

A simple pudding for outdoors or in, and quick to prepare. Ideal for children wanting to have a go at 'cooking'.

Ingredients to serve 4

2 bananas, peeled and thinly sliced
2 fresh ripe pears, peeled, cored and chopped into small pieces
125 g (4 oz) raisins
Juice of 1 lemon
200 ml (7 fl oz) double cream
70 g (2$^{1}/_{2}$ oz) slivered almonds
2 tablespoons clear honey
A few extra almonds and raisins for decoration

Method

Put the banana, pear and raisins into a mixing bowl, then squeeze in the lemon juice. Whisk the cream until stiff and then blend in the almonds and honey. Add the fruit with the lemon juice to the cream and honey mixture and blend in the ingredients. Spoon the mixture into glasses or bowls and chill in the refrigerator before serving.

When ready to serve, sprinkle the tops of the cream with raisins and almonds.

Hazelnut Meringue Gateau

Ingredients to 4–6

115 g (4 oz) toasted hazelnuts, skins rubbed off
4 egg whites
170 g (6 oz) caster sugar
225 ml (8 fl oz) whipping cream
Icing sugar for dusting

Method

Put the toasted hazelnuts into a liquidiser and finely grind to resemble breadcrumbs.

Whisk the egg whites until very stiff; beat in the caster sugar a spoonful at a time until well incorporated. Mix in the ground hazelnuts gently, taking care not to overmix.

Line two baking trays with a sheet of baking parchment; divide the meringue mixture between the two trays, spreading the mixture into a circle with a palette knife. Put into the centre of the oven at 170ºC/325ºF/gas mark 3. Bake the meringues for 30–40 minutes until the tops are crisp. Remove from the oven and transfer onto a wire rack to cool.

When required, whip the cream and sandwich the two circles of meringue together. Dust over icing sugar if wished.

Cook's note
Can be served with strawberry or raspberry purée.

Lemon and Yoghurt Soufflé

Using half yoghurt and half cream gives the soufflé a fresher, lighter texture and flavour. If you don't want the bother of making a soufflé pour the mixture into a bowl and present as a light mousse.

Ingredients to serve 4–6

Juice and finely grated rind of 2 lemons

225 g (8 oz) caster sugar

6 eggs, separated

4 sheets of leaf gelatine, soaked in cold water

50 ml (2 fl oz) boiling water (for gelatine)

150 ml (¼ pint) natural set plain yoghurt

150 ml (¼ pint) whipping cream

150 ml (¼ pint) whipping cream for decoration

Method

Tie a double layer of greaseproof paper around the outside of a soufflé dish with string, the paper rising about 7 cm (3 inches) above the dish.

Put the juice of ½ a lemon, and rind of both lemons, sugar and egg yolks into a large bowl; beat well together. Drop the soaked gelatine into the boiling water and stir until dissolved. Stir in the remaining lemon juice and then pour it into the sugar and egg mixture, and blend thoroughly together. Beat the yoghurt until smooth and then fold into the soufflé mixture. Beat the cream and fold into the soufflé mixture. Beat the egg whites until just holding shape, then fold into the soufflé mixture. Pile into the prepared soufflé dish if using and chill in the refrigerator.

When required, remove from the refrigerator and peel away the paper from the soufflé. Whip the cream, put into a piping bag and pipe 'rosettes' onto the top of the soufflé.

Fresh Pears Filled with Lavender and Honey Ice Cream

Called in at Hay castle and went with the four pretty girl archers to shoot and pick up their arrows in the field opposite the castle.

(Kilvert's Diaries, 26th June 1872)

And then on, we imagine to tea on the lawn at the vicarage. This is a perfect pudding for a summer's archery or tennis party.

Ingredients to serve 4

4 free-range egg yolks

4 teaspoons lavender sugar

300 ml (¹/₂ pint) single cream

6 tablespoons liquid lavender honey

300 ml (¹/₂ pint) double cream

4 ripe pears

Method

Put the egg yolks and sugar into a basin and beat until pale and fluffy. Stir in the single cream and honey, set the bowl over a pan of simmering water, or use a double saucepan and stir until the mixture thickens. Allow to cool, this can be done quickly by standing the basin in a bowl of cold water – ice cubes can also be added.

Whip the double cream and fold it into the cooled ice cream mixture. Put into a suitable container and freeze until required. Transfer from the freezer to the refrigerator 10 minutes before serving.

Peel 4 ripe pears, cut in half and the core removed. Lay the pears on a serving dish and pile a scoop of ice cream into the core cavity. Decorate with a small fresh flower and serve.

Cook's note
The type of honey will affect the flavour of the ice cream; just choose your favourite. Lavender ice cream is also great with sliced banana.

Pineapple and Lime Sorbet

'…in the heat of noon,
Only the croonings of the ring dove lull
The leafy woods.'

(*The Island* by Francis Brett Young in *Wild Wings and Some Footsteps,* J. Wentworth Day)

Combining lime with pineapple gives a refreshing and piquant sweet flavour. One hour before serving put the glasses into the refrigerator to chill and frost.

Ingredients to serve 6–8

1 small ripe pineapple
225 g (8 oz) caster sugar
300 ml ($^1/_2$ pint) cold water
Juice and grated rind of 3 limes
Juice of 1 small lemon

Method

Slice the top and bottom off the pineapple and reserve the best leaves for decoration, if desired. Cut the pineapple into thick slices and remove the skin and core. Cut the pineapple flesh into pieces, put into a food processor and liquidise to a smooth purée.

Heat the sugar and water in a saucepan until the sugar has dissolved, then simmer until reduced by a third. Remove from the heat and mix in the pineapple purée, add the lime juice and rind and lemon juice, blend well. Pour into a suitable container and freeze.

To serve Remove from the freezer 10–15 minutes before scraping with a spoon into the chilled, frosted glasses. Decorate with the reserved pineapple leaves.

Sherry Ice Cream and Brandy Snap Terrine

Oakley Court was on the Thames, and after a day's racing it was delightful to go on the river and laze about till dinner time. Trees and bushes over-hung the water providing many shady corners where punts and boats could hide discreetly and sheltered nooks for lovers to sit in peace and seclusion.

(Chit-Chat, Lady Augusta Fane)

Those were the days, when picnics were stylish and elegant, but they need not just be memories of the past. This pudding will lift any occasion out of the ordinary into a special event.

Ingredients to serve 6

600 ml (1 pint) double cream
150 ml ($^1/_4$ pint) cream sherry
90 g ($3^1/_4$ oz) icing sugar
6 brandy snaps, crushed
125 ml (4 fl oz) whipped cream for decoration

Method

Beat the double cream, gradually adding the sherry and sugar a little at a time. Beat until it just holds its shape in soft peaks. Line a loaf tin with greaseproof paper and pour in the sherry ice-cream mixture. Freeze until firm, remove from the freezer, turn out onto a board and, using a palette knife, press the crushed brandy snaps around the top and sides of the terrine. Place onto a serving dish and return to the freezer. Only remove the pudding from the freezer when readty to serve otherwise it will begin to melt and be too soft. If using, decorate with the whipped cream piped through a star nozzle and if desired, fresh fruit can be served as an accompaniment.

CAKES

Apricot Curd

Curds will keep for three to four weeks in the refrigerator, and are the ideal store cupboard ingredient for spreading on scones, toast or bread. Dried apricots are more concentrated in flavour than fresh ones, but they need to be soaked overnight.

Ingredients to make 1 kg (2 lb)

170 g (6 oz) dried apricots
250 g (9 oz) caster sugar
5 tablespoons butter
Grated rind and juice of 1 lemon
2 eggs, beaten

Method

Put the apricots into a bowl, cover with water and leave to soak for 24 hours.

Tip the soaked apricots into a saucepan with the water, bring to the boil and then simmer until soft – this takes about half an hour. When the fruit is soft, transfer to a liquidiser and blend until smooth. Put the fruit purée into the top of a double saucepan or into bowl standing over a saucepan of boiling water. Stir in the sugar, butter, lemon juice and rind. Turn down the heat, cover, and cook until the sugar has dissolved, stirring frequently. When the sugar has dissolved, remove the curd from the heat and mix in the beaten egg; return to the heat and cook gently until the curd coats the back of a spoon, stirring from time to time. Pot into clean warm jars and seal as normal.

Smoked Bacon Scone

Philippa made agitated signals to me; I cut her dead and went to ground in the tea tent.

(*Some Experiences of an Irish R. M.,* E. OE. Somerville and Martin Ross)

Ingredients to serve 4–6

115 g (4 oz) rindless smoked bacon, cut into small pieces

1 medium onion, peeled and finely chopped

3 sticks celery, washed and finely chopped

450 g (1 lb) self raising flour

1 teaspoon mustard powder

Sea salt and pepper to taste

100 g (3½ oz) margarine or butter

2 tablespoon parsley, chopped

1 beaten egg

300 ml (½ pint) milk

Method

Pre-heat the oven to 200ºC/400ºF/gas mark 6. Put the bacon into a non-stick frying pan and sauté until the fat begins to run, add the chopped onion and celery, fry for 5 minutes. Remove from the heat to cool.

In a mixing bowl, sift together the flour, mustard powder, salt and pepper to taste. Rub in the fat until the mixture resembles fine breadcrumbs. Add the chopped parsley and stir in the cooled, cooked bacon, onion and celery. Blend well together.

Beat the egg with the milk and pour into the scone mixture. Knead into a dough on a lightly floured board, taking care not to over-handle or the mixture will become too heavy. Grease a baking tray and shape the dough into a circle. Lightly mark into sections with the point of a knife. Bake in the pre-heated oven for 20–25 minutes.

Mrs Beeton's Tennis Cake

Long, lazy afternoons and tea on the lawn have long been associated with Wimbledon and private tennis parties. The days when the first lady tennis players wore elaborately flounced, ground-length dresses, high necks, ornamented sleeves and clinched waists are memories of the past, but tea in gardens and this cake can still be enjoyed – our unpredictable summer weather permitting.

(This recipe comes from the Wimbledon Lawn Tennis Museum)

Ingredients to serve 6

40 g (1¹/₂ oz) crystallised lemon or
  orange peel
115 g (4 oz) raisins
170 g (6 oz) butter, softened
170 g (6 oz) soft brown sugar

Juice and grated rind of 1 small lemon
4 medium eggs, beaten
225 g (8 oz) plain flour
25 g (1 oz) ground almonds

Method

Pre-heat the oven to 180ºC/350ºF/gas mark 4. Prepare an 18-cm (7-inch) round. cake tin. Line the bottom of the tin with a circle of greaseproof paper.

Roughly chop the crystallised orange or lemon peel and the raisins. Cream the butter and sugar together until pale and fluffy; stir in the lemon juice and grated rind; add half the quantity of the beaten egg.

Sieve the flour and put 2 tablespoons into the creamed butter and sugar and lemon mixture, stir in the ground almonds and the remaining beaten egg. Fold in the remaining flour and the chopped raisins. Mix well together. Pile into the prepared cake tin and bake in the pre-heated oven for 1 hour and then lower the temperature to 160ºC/325ºF/gas mark 3 and bake for a further 30 minutes until the cake is firm to the touch.

When cooked, remove from the oven and allow to cool in the tin before turning out.

Peach and Almond Cake

'Won't you take a little refreshment?' asked Mr Springwheat; in the hearty way these hospitable fellows welcomed everybody. 'Yes I will,' replied Sponge, turning to the sideboard as though it were an inn.

(Mr Sponge's Sporting Tour, R. S. Surtees)

Ripe peaches are essential for this cake, which can be served with whipped cream flavoured with peach liqueur for a pudding, or on its own for tea or supper.

Ingredients to make a 20-cm (8-inch) cake

2 large or 3 small ripe peaches, skin and stones removed
Juice of $^1/_2$ lemon
140 g (5 oz) plain flour with a pinch of salt
$1^1/_2$ level teaspoons baking powder
70 g (3 oz) caster sugar
55 g (2 oz) butter
2 large eggs, beaten
4 tablespoons Kirsch
55 g (2 oz) lightly toasted almonds

For the glaze
1 tablespoon apricot jam
4 tablespoons water
Splash of Kirsch

Method

Pre-heat the oven to 180ºC/350ºF/gas mark 4. Line a 20-cm (8-inch) cake tin with baking parchment and brush with melted butter. Cut the peaches into pieces and put into a bowl, sprinkle over the lemon juice. Turn the peaches in the juice to prevent discolouration.

Sift the salted flour with the baking powder in a separate bowl, stir in the sugar and make a well in the centre. Melt the butter and pour into the well, add the beaten egg and the Kirsch. Blend all the ingredients well together and then fold in the almonds and peach pieces.

Pour the mixture into the prepared cake tin and bake for 1 hour until cooked through and firm to the touch. If after the first half hour of cooking the top of the cake is browning well, lower the oven temperature by a few degrees for the remaining 30 minutes.

To make the glaze. Simmer together the apricot jam, water and Kirsch, sieve out any lumps.

Remove the cake from the oven and allow to cool. When cooled, turn the cake out of the tin and peel away the lining parchment. Brush the cake with the apricot glaze.

Cook's note
Stoned cherries can be used as an alternative to peaches.

Banana and Pine Kernel Cake

This recipe is a good one for children to make during the summer holidays. The bananas need to be over-ripe, as they give the cake a good strong flavour. Not over-sweet, it has a buttery, brioche-like texture so it can accompany savoury salads as well as being a tea-time treat.

Ingredients to serve 6–8

2 tablespoons cream cheese

2 very ripe bananas, peeled

Grated rind and juice of 1 small
  lemon

170 g (6 oz) self raising flour

$^1/_2$ teaspoon bicarbonate of soda

$^1/_2$ teaspoon ground cinnamon

A good pinch of salt

140 g (5 oz) caster sugar

100 g ($3^1/_2$ oz) softened butter or
  margarine

1 large egg, beaten

100 g ($3^1/_2$ oz) pine kernels

Method

Pre-heat the oven to 180ºC/350ºF/gas mark 4 Line a 740 g (1³/₄ lb) loaf tin or 2 smaller tins with baking parchment.

Mash together, cream cheese, bananas, grated rind and lemon juice until smooth and free of lumps. In a separate bowl, sift the flour with the bicarbonate of soda, cinnamon and salt. Cream together in another bowl the sugar and butter or margarine until light and fluffy; add the beaten egg a little at a time, beating as you go. Put a tablespoon of banana mixture into the sugar and butter, add a tablespoon of sifted dry ingredients and gently fold in. Repeat this process until all ingredients are used up and then fold in the pine kernels. Pour into the prepared tin(s).

Bake in the pre-heated oven for 40–45 minutes. Test by inserting a skewer in the centre of the cake – if it comes away clean it is done. Should the cake be browning too quickly on top and not cooked in the centre, cover the top with kitchen foil to prevent further browning.

Remove from the oven, cool a little in the tin before turning out onto a wire rack to cool.

Autumn

SOUPS

Carrot and Coriander Soup

Mrs Beeton tells us that garden carrots were first introduced in the reign of Elizabeth I. They were so highly esteemed, that fashionable ladies wore the leaves in their headdresses.

Ingredients to serve 4

40 g (1$\frac{1}{2}$ oz) unsalted butter
100 ml (3$\frac{1}{2}$ fl oz) olive or vegetable oil
450 g (1 lb) carrots, peeled and finely chopped
1 large onion, peeled and chopped
1 clove garlic, crushed
900 ml (1$\frac{1}{2}$ pints) vegetables or chicken stock
10 coriander seeds
1 bay leaf
Sea salt and freshly ground black pepper
90 ml (3$\frac{1}{2}$ fl oz) double cream

Method

Melt the butter with the oil in a large saucepan, add the carrot, onion and garlic. Cover and 'sweat' the vegetables until soft. Pour in the stock, add the coriander seeds, bay leaf and seasonings to taste, and simmer for 25 minutes. Remove from the heat and allow to cool slightly. Discard the bay leaf and pour the soup into a food processor. Blend until smooth and transfer to a clean saucepan. Stir in the cream and re-heat to serve.

Chestnut and Smoked Bacon Soup

Some good advice from Mr Facey Romford: 'Happy are they who go out to please themselves, and not to astonish others.'

(*Mr Facey Romford's Hounds,* R. S. Surtees)

Ingredients to serve 4

4 tablespoons vegetable oil

85 g (3 oz) chopped smoked bacon, rind removed

2 onions, peeled and finely chopped

1 clove garlic, crushed

300 ml (^{1}/$_2$ pint) chicken or vegetable stock

170 g (6 oz) peeled chestnuts (fresh or frozen)

Sea salt and freshly ground black pepper to taste

300 ml (^{1}/$_2$ pint) single cream

Fried bread croutons (optional)

1 teaspoon parsley, chopped

Method

Heat the oil in a saucepan and fry the chopped bacon until the fat begins to run. With a slotted spoon (so the fat is left in the saucepan), remove the pieces of bacon and put to one side. Put the chopped onion into the saucepan and cook until soft. Add the garlic, stock, chestnuts, salt and pepper to taste, and simmer for 10–15 minutes. Remove from the heat, allow to cool a little and then liquidise until smooth. Return the soup to the pan, stir in the chopped bacon and cream, re-heat, and serve with the fried bread croutons if used and sprinkle over the chopped parsley.

Cook's note
To save time, use ready-cooked, frozen or vacuum-packed chestnuts. (Tinned chestnuts will not have such a fresh taste.)

Curried Pumpkin Soup

'Put off the dinner (wheeze); put off the dinner (puff),' repeated he, blowing furiously into his clean shirt-frill, which stuck up under his nose like a hand-saw, 'put off the dinner (wheeze); put off the dinner (puff); I wish you wouldn't do such things without consulting (gasp) me…' Well, but, my dear, you know hunters are always allowed a little law,' observed Mrs Jog.

(*Mr Sponge's Sporting Tour,* R. S. Surtees)

This soup will happily wait if dinner has to be put off for a time, though cooks too, can be a law unto themselves as well as hunters.

Ingredients to serve 4–6

4 tablespoons olive oil

2 medium onions

675 g (1^1/$_2$ lb) pumpkin flesh, skin and seeds discarded

750 ml (1^1/$_4$ pints) chicken or vegetable stock

1 clove garlic, crushed

2–3 teaspoons curry paste

Sea salt and freshly ground black pepper

150 ml (^{1}/$_4$ pint) single cream

Method

Heat the oil in a large saucepan. Add the onion and cook until soft, then put in the pumpkin flesh and stir well. Lower the heat and cook for 2 minutes, stirring to prevent sticking. Pour in the stock. Mix in the crushed garlic, curry paste, season to taste and simmer for approximately 20 minutes until the pumpkin is cooked. When ready, remove from the heat and allow to cool a little. Transfer to a food processor and blend until smooth. Return the blended soup to the saucepan and stir in the cream, reserving a little to swirl. Check the seasonings, re-heat if necessary, but do not boil. Serve with a swirl of cream on top if desired.

Hunter's Soup

The huntsman winds his horn.
The huntsman winds his horn.
And a hunting we will go
A hunting we will go.

(*A Hunting We Will Go,* from Coridon's
Song and other Verses)

A country soup made from any leftover pieces of game, ideal for warming up your guests after a day in the open when appetites match the generosity of your biggest soup bowls.

Ingredients to serve 4–6

55 g (2 oz) beef dripping

115 g (4 oz) streaky bacon rind removed and chopped

1 large onion, peeled and chopped

1 large carrot, peeled and thinly sliced

4 sticks celery, washed and finely chopped

1 litre (1³/₄ pints) game stock

300 ml (¹/₂ pint) red wine

Sea salt and black pepper to taste

170 g (6 oz) cooked pieces of game

Method

Melt the dripping in a large pan and put in the chopped bacon. Fry until the fat begins to run and then add the chopped onion, carrot and celery. Pour in the stock, red wine and season to taste. Simmer gently for ³/₄ –1 hour and then add the game pieces. Slacken the potato flour with a little cold water, stir well and stir into the soup until the soup thickens slightly.

Cook's note
The flavour of the soup depends upon the quality of the stock and the dripping from a joint of roast beef saved from Sunday lunch. Vegetable oil can be used instead of dripping but the flavour will not be quite so good.

Roasted Garlic and Marrow Soup

Ingredients to serve 6

1 whole head garlic

50 ml (2 fl oz) olive oil

60 g (2¼ oz) butter

1 medium onion, peeled and finely chopped

1 small marrow peeled, cut in half, seeds
  removed

900 ml (1½ pints) chicken or vegetable stock

Sea salt and freshly ground black pepper

150 ml (¼ pint) double cream

Small bunch fresh chives, finely chopped

Method

Pre-heat the oven to 200ºC/400ºF/gas mark 6. Break the garlic into individual cloves, remove the centre stalk and root; do not remove the skin. Put the garlic into a roasting tin and pour over the oil. Roast in the pre-heated oven for 15–20 minutes until soft and brown. Poke with the point of a knife to test for softness. When ready, remove from the oven and allow to cool sufficiently to handle. With the back of a knife, press the garlic from its skin, put the pulp to one side and discard the skin.

    Melt the butter in a large saucepan, add the onion and cook until soft.

    Cut the marrow into cubes and put with the onion in the pan. Pour in the stock, add the crushed garlic, season well to taste, cover and cook gently until the marrow is soft. Remove the pan from the heat, allow to cool a little and then liquidise until smooth. Return the soup to a clean saucepan, stir in the cream and chopped chives. Heat when required, but it mustn't be allowed to boil.

Cook's note
The garlic can be roasted and prepared to the 'pulp' stage in advance and kept in a small jar in the refrigerator until required.

Tomato and Orange Soup

Lie low and let the punt ride, a sliding creature of wave and wind.

(Wild Wings and Some Footsteps, J. Wentworth Day)

A quick and easy soup, but to save even more time, a tin of chopped tomatoes can be used, though the flavour will not be quite as strong. It is also a very good soup for taking in a flask for those long waits when out on the river banks, moors or marshes.

Ingredients to serve 4

900 g (2 lb) fresh ripe tomatoes, skinned,
  seeded and chopped

2 tablespoons olive oil

2 medium onions, peeled and finely chopped

1 carrot, peeled and finely chopped

1 small clove garlic, crushed

1 tablespoon tomato paste

600 ml (1 pint) chicken or vegetable stock

Grated rind and juice of 1 orange

1 teaspoon organic brown cane sugar

Sea salt and cayenne pepper to taste

1 tablespoon fresh basil leaves, chopped

Method

To skin tomatoes Put the tomatoes into a large bowl and pour over boiling water. Leave to stand for a few minutes then drain off the water. The skin should come away easily using a pointed knife. The tomato core can be put through a fine sieve to remove seeds if desired.

Heat the oil in a saucepan and fry the onion and carrot until just softening. Put in the garlic, tomatoes, tomato paste, stock, orange rind and juice. Season to taste and simmer for 20 minutes. Remove from the heat and allow to cool a little. Transfer to a food processor and liquidise until smooth. Return the soup to the saucepan and re-heat. Serve with a sprinkling of chopped fresh basil leaves.

STARTERS AND SIDE-DISHES

Bacon and Herb Potato Patties

Be very careful when and where you appear in plus fours; if in doubt, don't…they should be worn by someone 'doing something active' in the country…Shorts are considered unsuitable except for certain games and seaside pastimes: on the whole they are out of favour.

(*The Pleasure of Your Company*, June and Doris Langley Moore)

As with this advice for country clothes, breakfast too has gone out of fashion although many like to have even a small breakfast before setting off for the day. These patties can be made in advance and stored for up to two days in the refrigerator. They just need re-heating when required and are also delicious served with sausages and fried egg – if you have time.

4 tablespoons olive oil

6 shallots, peeled and finely chopped

115 g (4 oz) rindless, smoked streaky bacon, chopped into small pieces

1 tablespoon parsley, chopped

450 g (1 lb) potatoes, boiled and mashed, seasoned with black pepper

170 g (6 oz) Parmesan cheese, finely grated

Sea salt to taste

$^1/_4$ teaspoon cayenne pepper

$^1/_4$ teaspoon grated nutmeg

1 egg, beaten

A little four for dusting before frying

1–2 tablespoon oil for frying

Method

Heat the olive oil in a frying pan and cook the shallots until just softening; add the bacon and fry until done. Put in the parsley, stir for a few seconds, remove from the heat and tip into a bowl. Add the mashed potato, grated cheese, salt, cayenne pepper and nutmeg. Blend well together and then bind with the beaten egg. Form into patties and dust each with a little flour. If not required immediately, store in a suitable container in the refrigerator.

When required, heat the patties in the oil and fry until golden brown on both sides.

Clotted Cream and Caviar Savoury

A friend of ours ordered no less than a pound of caviar for a dinner party and, having no ice-box, placed it in a basin in her stone pantry sink so it would keep cool overnight. The next morning the kitchen maid informed her that she had thrown away 'a lot of nasty black grease which the master must have brought in from his motor-car'.

(*The Pleasure of Your Company*, June and Doris Langely Moore)

If Russian caviar is beyond the weekly shopping budget, Onuga caviar is a good alternative and a fraction of the cost being made from pasteurised golden herring roe and containing no preservatives. This recipe is very quick to make, excellent as either a savoury instead of a pudding, or for a speedy light lunch served by itself or with a green salad.

Ingredients to serve 4

55 g (2 oz) pot Onuga or lumpfish caviar
4 tablespoons clotted cream
4 crumpets

Method

Blend the caviar into the clotted cream and refrigerate to chill and set. When ready to eat, toast the crumpets and while still hot, spread the chilled caviar cream onto each crumpet.

Double Cooked Roquefort Soufflé

A really good recipe for entertaining: it can be made in advance then put into the oven to re-heat and rise when required. The soufflés keep well refrigerated for 2–3 days after the first cooking.

Ingredients to serve 6–8 depending on depth of ramekin

Small knob of melted butter for greasing ramekins
50 g (1³/₄ oz) butter
50 g (1³/₄ oz) plain flour
300 ml (¹/₂ pint) whole milk
125 g (4¹/₂ oz) Roquefort cheese
3 eggs, separated
¹/₄ teaspoon ground mace
Sea salt and freshly ground black pepper to taste
Single cream and grated Parmesan for serving

Method

Brush the ramekins with the melted butter; place a circle of baking parchment in the bottom of each ramekin. Melt the butter in a saucepan and add the flour. Cook until the mixture lightens then remove from the heat.

Pour the milk gradually into the mixture beating as you go. Return to the heat and cook until the mixture thickens. Remove from the heat; blend in the Roquefort cheese, egg yolks, mace, salt and pepper to taste.

Blend well together by hand or put into a food processor and blend until smooth.

Pre-heat the oven to 180ºC/350ºF/gas mark 4. Whisk the egg whites and with a metal spoon fold into the Roquefort mixture. Fill the ramekins with the soufflé mixture, not quite to the top. Stand the ramekins in a roasting tin and pour in boiling water until it reaches halfway up the sides of the ramekins. Bake in the pre-heated oven for approximately 15–20 minutes until pale and golden.

Remove the ramekins from the roasting tin and allow to cool. Run a knife around the edge of each soufflé to loosen then turn out onto a dish. Cover, and keep in the refrigerator until required.

When ready to serve, heat the oven to 220ºC/425ºF/gas mark 7. Pour a little single cream over each soufflé, season with sea salt and black pepper. Sprinkle over a little grated Parmesan and bake for 10–12 minutes, until risen and golden brown.

Serving suggestion Hazelnut and green leaf salad tossed in hazelnut oil, or use walnuts with walnut oil.

Mushrooms with Garlic and Chicken Liver Pâté

I like an autumn wold, and a wood where summer's done,
And white hounds and limber, to sing through its timber
The melody, the melody that makes the red fox run.

(*Wild Wings and Some Footsteps,* J. Wentworth Day – poem
by Patrick R. Chalmers)

Field mushrooms grow well in horse-grazed pastures, if you have the inclination to rise early, which is the best time to gather mushrooms. If not, supermarkets and grocers sell them during the autumn season.

Ingredients to serve 4

8 large open-capped field mushrooms
2 tablespoons olive oil
2 cloves garlic, crushed

For the pâté
70 g (2¹/₂ oz) unsalted butter
4 rashers streaky bacon, rind removed,
  chopped

1 small onion, peeled and chopped
1 clove garlic, crushed
450 g (1 lb) chicken livers
2 teaspoons tomato paste
2 teaspoons English mustard
Sea salt and freshly ground black pepper to
  taste

Method

For the mushrooms Peel the skin from the mushroom caps. Remove the stalks, chop finely and reserve for the pâté. Mix together the oil and crushed garlic and toss the mushroom caps in the oil until well covered. Leave to soak in the oil while you make the pâté.

For the pâté Melt half the butter in a deep-sided frying pan, put in the bacon and fry until the fat begins to run and then add the chopped onion, crushed garlic and chopped mushroom stems and cook for a few minutes. Tip the contents of the pan into a food processor. Put the remaining half of butter into the frying pan and cook the chicken livers until just cooked through, and no longer pink. Put into the food processor with the bacon and onion mixture. Add the tomato paste, mustard, seasonings to taste and blend until smooth and creamy.

Pre-heat the oven to 180ºC/350ºF/gas mark 4. Lay the oil-soaked mushroom caps on a baking tray and evenly divide the pâté into each cap. Bake in the oven for 20–25 minutes – time will depend on the size of mushroom caps. Serve straight from the oven on a slice of fried bread, warm ciabatta or toast.

Potted Pheasant with Crab Apple Jelly

May the wing of friendship never moult a feather

(Dick Swiveller's sentiment, The Old Curiosity Shop,
Charles Dickens)

Ingredients to serve 4

450 g (1 lb) cooked pheasant

150 ml (¹/₄ pint) jellied game stock

50 ml (2 fl oz) Amontillado sherry or tawny port

1 teaspoon ground nutmeg

1 small clove garlic, crushed

Sea salt and cayenne pepper to taste

Method

Put the pheasant meat into a food processor and whiz until finely chopped. Turn out into a mixing bowl. Melt the jellied stock in a saucepan, remove from the heat, pour in the sherry or port and allow the liquid to cool before pouring over the minced pheasant. Mix in the nutmeg, crushed garlic, salt and cayenne pepper. Blend well together and press the mixture into a pâté dish or individual ramekins. Serve with the crab apple jelly (see page 168), toast or warm crusty bread.

FISH

Cod Roasted with a Cheese and Herb Crust

Cooking is an art, and so is eating. If we don't know how to cook, we're not likely to know how to eat.

(The Complete Life, John Erskine)

Ingredients to serve 4

550 g (1¹/₄ lb) cod, cut into 4 pieces
85 g (3 oz) wholemeal breadcrumbs
55 g (2 oz) Parmesan cheese
6 tablespoons olive oil
8 anchovy fillets, chopped
1 medium onion, peeled and chopped
2 tablespoons tarragon leaves, chopped
¹/₄ teaspoon cayenne pepper
Sea salt and ground black pepper to taste

Method

Pre-heat the oven to 190ºC/375ºF/gas mark 5. Heat the oil in a saucepan and put in the onion, cook until soft. Remove from the heat and add all the rest of the ingredients except for the fish, mix well together.

Place the cod pieces on a baking tray and divide cheese and herb mixture into 4 and place each portion onto a piece of fish, pressing the mixture firmly onto the fish. Bake in the pre-heated oven for 15–20 minutes.

Devilled Crab

A southerly wind and a cloudy sky
A hunting morn proclaim
And Felix Fox is up and dressed
Leaving his wife to do the rest.
Felix they greet with loud hooray!
He trusts they'll proceed without delay,
While he is carving his wife appears,
'Don't stir,' she says; 'How d'ye do, my dears!'

(*The Hunt Breakfast, The Foxes Frolic;*
Sir Francis Burnand)

A hot and spicy dish, and very easy to prepare. There will be no delay with this unusual breakfast dish, though it is just as good as a starter for lunch or dinner. If you haven't got real scallop shells, use ovenproof gratin dishes.

1 onion, peeled and finely chopped

3 cooked, dressed crabs, any shell pieces removed

140 g (4½ oz) brown breadcrumbs

85 g (3 oz) butter

1 tablespoon Worcestershire sauce

3 teaspoons tomato paste

Juice and grated rind of 1 lemon

1 tablespoon anchovy essence

125 ml (4 fl oz) single cream

4 teaspoons curry paste

6 small knobs of butter for grilling

Method

Melt the butter in a saucepan, add the onion and cook until soft and then tip the contents of the pan into a mixing bowl. Add all the other ingredients except the 6 knobs of butter to the onion and mix thoroughly together. Divide the mixture between the six dishes or shells. With a fork, spread evenly, taking care not to press too firmly. Dot the knobs of butter on top of each portion and brown under a moderate grill until the centre is heated through and the top golden brown.

Kipper Cakes

The family tea-meal is very like breakfast only with more cakes and knicknackery.

(Mrs Beeton)

Many people after a day in the saddle or working in the open air, like something for tea or supper that can be prepared quickly. These kipper cakes are ideal for just such an occasion. They can be made in advance, retrieved from the refrigerator and pan-fried in minutes. Kipper cakes can also be served as a first course.

Ingredients for 4–6 cakes

1 pack kipper fillets

2 medium potatoes, boiled

2 eggs

25 g (1 oz) knob softened butter

2 teaspoons parsley, chopped

Ground black pepper to taste

Cayenne pepper to taste

2 tablespoons brown breadcrumbs

Olive oil for frying

Method

Boil the kippers until cooked; remove them from the bag and leave to cool before flaking the flesh and removing any skin and bones.

Mix the flaked kipper with the mashed potato, stir in the softened butter and one egg. Add the chopped parsley, black and cayenne pepper to taste and mix together thoroughly. Divide the mixture into 4 or 6 pieces and form into cakes. Beat the remaining egg and dip the kipper cakes into it until well coated. Coat the egg-dipped kipper cakes with the breadcrumbs, then wrap in cling film and refrigerate until needed.

When required, heat the oil in a frying pan and fry the kipper cakes on both sides until golden brown.

Fillets of Plaice with Lime and Basil Butter Sauce

Bicycles gradually became the chief vehicles for ladies paying calls. They would even tuck up their trains and ride out to dinner on them. One summer evening my parents rode ten miles to dine at Six Mile Bottom; their evening clothes were carried in cases on the handlebars; for of course, you couldn't possibly dine without dressing.

(Gwen Raverat, recalling her Cambridge childhood in *Carriages at Eight*, Frank E.Huggett)

This delicious supper dish is suitable as a first course or main, using one large or two small fillets per person for a main course and one fillet per person for a starter. The sauce is refreshing and pleases the eye as well as the taste buds.

Ingredients to serve 4 as a starter, 2 as a main course

For the sauce:
Grated rind and juice of 1 large lime
125 ml (4 fl oz) fish stock or water
4 tablespoons dry vermouth
1 teaspoon clear honey
115 g (4 oz) unsalted butter cut into small cubes
10 leaves fresh basil, cut into pieces
100 ml (3^1/$_2$ fl oz) double cream
Sea salt and freshly ground black pepper to taste

* * *

2 large or 4 small fresh plaice fillets
2–4 small knobs of butter for grilling
Sea salt and freshly ground black pepper to taste
A few fresh basil leaves and lime slices to garnish

Method

To make the sauce Put the grated rind and juice of the lime into a saucepan, pour in the stock or water, vermouth and honey, stir and bring to the boil. Simmer until reduced by approximately one-third. Reduce the heat to very low and whisk in the butter, a piece at a time, until well blended in. The sauce must not boil. Add the basil leaves and mix in the cream. Season to taste.

For the fish Put the fillet skin-side down on a grill pan, pour a small amount of water into the bottom of the pan. Dot each fillet with the knobs of butter. Season to taste and grill for 2–3 minutes on each side.

To serve Peel away the fish skin, lay the fillets onto serving plates and spoon over the warm lime and basil sauce.

Stuffed River Trout with Almond Sauce

Caleb the shepherd from W. H. Hudson's *A Shepherd's Life*, owned a large tabby cat which never wanted to be fed…Behind Caleb's cottage was a piece of waste ground which led down to the river. One day, Caleb came upon his cat eating something among the weeds, it was a good-sized trout, freshly caught. The surrounding area was littered with fins, heads and portions of backbone. Caleb did not tell a soul, but would watch the cat every day bring a fresh trout to that spot and eat it. How the cat caught the fish, remained a mystery.

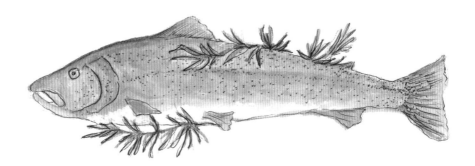

Ingredients to serve 4

4 good-sized trout, cleaned, gutted, heads
   removed
Large piece of buttered kitchen foil

For the filling

55 g (2 oz) unsalted butter
1 small carrot, peeled and finely chopped
1 stick celery, washed and chopped
1 medium onion, peeled and chopped
1 tablespoon parsley, freshly chopped
1 tablespoon tarragon, freshly chopped
85 g (3 oz) wholemeal breadcrumbs

Juice and grated rind of 1 small lemon
1 egg, beaten
Sea salt and freshly ground black pepper, to
   taste

For the sauce

25 g (1 oz) unsalted butter
85 g (3 oz) flaked almonds
150 ml (¼ pint) single cream
1 tablespoon tarragon, chopped
Sea salt and freshly ground black pepper, to
   taste

Method

To make the filling Melt the butter in a saucepan, add the chopped vegetables and cook until soft. Remove from the heat, add the chopped herbs, breadcrumbs, lemon juice and rind, seasonings to taste and bind together with the beaten egg.

Pre-heat the oven to 200ºC/400ºF/gas mark 6. Fill each trout with the vegetable mixture and lay them on four pieces of buttered kitchen foil. Lay another piece of foil over the top of each trout and wrap around the trout to form a parcel, crimping the edges to seal. Place the fish parcels on a baking tray, put into the pre-heated oven and cook for 20 minutes or slightly longer if the trout are very large.

To make the sauce Melt the butter in a saucepan, put in the almonds and cook until lightly browned. Stir in the cream and tarragon, season to taste. Leave in the pan while the cooked trout is removed from the oven. Unwrap the trout parcels and pour any fish liquid into the sauce.

To serve Place each trout on a warmed dinner plate and pour the sauce over.

Cook's note
If you have the time and inclination, the skin can be removed from the trout before serving.

MAIN COURSES

Chicken and Herb Patties

I knew a fox who slept day after day in a straw stack at the back of a hen house, in a farmyard.

He never killed a hen in that farmyard.

(*Wild Wings and Some Footsteps,* J. Wentworth Day)

A good recipe for using up left-over roast chicken. Alternatively, chicken can be bought from supermarkets ready cooked.

Ingredients to make 4–6 small patties

1 tablespoon olive oil	$^1/_2$ teaspoon ground nutmeg
450 g (1 lb) cooked and minced chicken	115 g (4 oz) white breadcrumbs
1 large onion, peeled and chopped	1 clove garlic, crushed
1 teaspoon parsley, chopped	Sea salt and black pepper to taste
1 teaspoon tarragon, chopped	2 eggs, beaten

Method

Heat the oil in a pan and sauté the onion until soft. Remove from the heat and allow to cool. Combine all the other ingredients together in a large bowl and add the cooled onion. Blend together thoroughly then form into round flat patties and put into the refrigerator to chill. When required, fry in hot fat for approximately 7 minutes on both sides until golden brown.

Drambuie Duck with Orange Sauce

It is during the green pea season that duck is usually found on the English table.

(Mrs Beeton)

Peas are the traditional accompaniment to duck, even though November is, or rather was before supermarkets made duck available for most of the year, the proper duck season.

This dish is quite straightforward to prepare, and the duck is sautéed beforehand to seal in the juices. No fat is required as sautéing the duck breasts skin-side down first, releases the meat's own fat. The duck is then baked in the oven with the sauce.

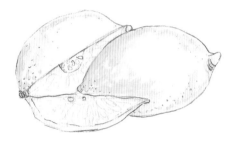

Ingredients to serve 6

6 boneless duck breasts
2 medium onions, peeled and finely chopped
1 clove garlic, crushed
125 ml (4 fl oz) Balsamic vinegar
90 g (3$^{1}/_{4}$ oz) Acacia honey
300 ml ($^{1}/_{2}$ pint) game or beef stock
Grated rind and juice of 2 medium oranges
Juice of $^{1}/_{2}$ lemon
175 ml (6 fl oz) Drambuie liqueur
2 tablespoons cornflour mixed with 180 ml (6 fl oz) cold water
Sea salt and freshly ground black pepper to taste
Orange slices and chopped parsley for decoration

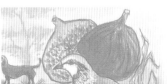

Method

Pre-heat the oven to 180ºC/350ºF/gas mark 4. Put in the duck breasts skin-side down in a heavy-based frying pan and seal until brown on both sides. Remove from the pan and set aside.

Put the onion and garlic into the frying pan and cook until the onion is soft and then add the vinegar and honey. Simmer until the mixture becomes syrupy. Pour in the stock, add the orange rind, orange and lemon juice and simmer for a further 5 minutes. Stir in the Drambuie and slackened cornflour. Continue to stir and cook until the sauce begins to thicken. Season to taste. Put the duck breasts, skin-side up, into an ovenproof dish and pour over the sauce. Cook uncovered in the pre-heated oven for 20–25 minutes. Timing will depend upon the thickness of the duck breasts – if small and thin, test after 15 minutes.

When cooked, remove from the oven, slice the duck breast and arrange on a warm serving dish. Pour the sauce over the meat and decorate with twists of orange slices and chopped parsley.

Serving suggestion Spinach, peas and creamed potatoes.

Lamb Fillet in Puff Pastry with Shrewsbury Sauce

The best fillets are cut from a leg of lamb, Scottish, English or Welsh being better in flavour and quality. Being wrapped in pastry, the meat needs to be of the best quality, as this dish requires fast cooking. It makes a perfect dinner party main course, as everything can be done beforehand and kept in the refrigerator and then be cooked in the oven and kept warm until required.

Ingredients to serve 4

4 lamb fillets approximately 115 g (4 oz) each
1 tablespoon olive oil
225 g (8 oz) puff pastry
1 small egg, beaten

For the sauce

50 g (1³/₄ oz) beef dripping
3 rashers smoked streaky bacon, chopped
1 carrot, peeled and finely chopped
1 onion, peeled and chopped
2 sticks celery, washed and chopped
1 tablespoon plain flour
240 ml (8¹/₂ fl oz) red wine
600 ml (1 pint) beef stock
2 teaspoons tomato paste
1 sprig each of rosemary, thyme and parsley tied together
2 tablespoons redcurrant jelly

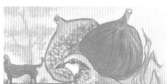

Method

Remove any surplus fat from the fillets. Heat the oil in a frying pan and seal the fillets in the hot oil on both sides until brown. Remove from the pan. Season the fillets with sea salt and freshly ground black pepper to taste and leave them to cool completely. Roll out the pastry into four 10-cm (4-inch) squares and place a fillet onto each square. Moisten the edges with the beaten egg and fold the edges over to form a parcel. Make a small hole in the top, lay on a baking tray and put in the refrigerator to 'rest' until required.

To make the sauce Melt the dripping in a saucepan and fry the chopped bacon. Add the chopped vegetables and cook until just softening. Blend in the flour and cook, stirring continuously, until the vegetables are golden brown – this will take between 5–10 minutes. Remove from the heat and blend in the red wine, stock and tomato paste then drop in the herbs. Season to taste and return to a low heat. Simmer gently for 1 hour.

After that time, strain the sauce into a clean saucepan, add the red currant jelly and heat to dissolve the jelly. Re-heat when required.

When ready to cook the lamb, pre-heat the oven to 220ºC/425ºF/gas mark 7. Brush the parcels with the beaten egg and cook for 20–25 minutes until the pastry is golden brown.

Cook's note
Cooking time may vary according to taste, some liking their lamb pinker than others: if this is the case, lower the temperature for the last 5–10 minutes of cooking time.

Pork Cutlets with Apple Mayonnaise

A well dressed cabby, the hay day of coaching era, was thought to have aristocratic origins, though he had really been a tailor before becoming a cab driver and so was known as 'King of the Cabmen'. When the police refused to let him park his cab outside his favourite coffee shop, started to dine in the West End instead, spreading a snow-white tablecloth on top of his cab from which he sometimes ate a splendid dinner sent out by sympathetic members of a nearby gentleman's club.

(*Carriages at Eight*, Frank E. Huggett)

Cutlets were a great favourite with the Victorians. This dish would be just right for eating off the top of a handsome cab or, indeed anywhere, being served cold with this slightly unusual apple mayonnaise using apple marmalade (see page 167)

Ingredients to serve 4

4 pork cutlets, fat and bone trimmed away	2 tablespoons Dijon mustard
85 g (3 oz) unsalted butter	Sea salt and freshly ground black pepper to
300 ml (¹/₂ pint) mayonnaise	taste
300 ml (¹/₂ pint) apple marmalade	1 tablespoon chopped parsley for garnishing

Method

Melt the butter in a frying pan and pan-fry the cutlets for 7–10 minutes on each side, time depending upon the thickness of the cutlets. Remove from the pan and place on a board, cover with another board and put a heavy weight on top to flatten the cutlets. Leave the cutlets to become cold.

Put the mayonnaise into a bowl, stir in the apple marmalade, mustard and seasonings.

Arrange the cooled cutlets down the centre of a serving dish and coat with the apple mayonnaise. Sprinkle over the chopped parsley.

Serving suggestion Boiled minted potatoes and a Waldorf salad.

Farmhouse Rabbit Stew with Raisins

Rabbits are available all year; domesticated rabbits sold in the shops have a similar flavour to chicken; wild rabbit often have a gamey flavour. Rabbit meat can be quite dry, which is why we have used the mix of oil and butter to give succulence and flavour. Stews are very satisfying, requiring no frills and usually no starter is needed.

Ingredients to serve 2

For the marinade

300 ml (¹/₂ pint) red wine

2 tablespoons red wine vinegar

Bouquet garni

3 teaspoons black peppercorns, crushed

For cooking

1 rabbit, skinned and jointed

1 rounded tablespoon plain flour seasoned
    with a little cayenne pepper and salt

3–4 tablespoons olive oil

55 g (2 oz) unsalted butter

1 large onion, peeled and chopped

150 ml (¹/₄ pint) chicken or vegetable stock

125 g (4¹/₂ oz) raisins soaked in a little tawny
    port

2 teaspoons redcurrant jelly

3 teaspoons crushed black peppercorns

Method

Mix all the marinade ingredients in a large bowl and put in the jointed rabbit. Cover and marinate for 1–2 days, turning occasionally.

When ready to cook, remove the rabbit from the marinade and pat dry with kitchen paper; reserve the marinade for cooking.

Dust the rabbit with the seasoned flour, heat the oil and butter in a large saucepan and sauté the rabbit until well browned all over. Remove the rabbit from the pan and sauté the onion. Return the rabbit to the pan and stir in the stock, the marinade, soaked raisins and redcurrant jelly. Season to taste, cover and simmer for 45–50 minutes until the rabbit is tender. Remove the bouquet garni, and then simmer until the cooking juices have reduced a little to concentrate the flavours. Check the seasonings and serve.

Game Pie

Well can we recall the monster hearth and fire at Farnborough, where, at first, unable to find our fingers to unbutton our coats, we broke in, half frozen…

(*The Coaching Age,* Stanley Harris)

This is one of the best English dishes that will not fail, the contents being cooked beforehand. The pie will also wait in a warm oven for late or delayed arrivals and will be very much appreciated, especially if guests are wet through and half frozen after a day in open country.

Ingredients to serve 4–6

2.5 kg (5 lb 8 oz) mixed game. i.e. rabbit, pheasant and venison

4 tablespoons flour seasoned with sea salt and cayenne pepper

4–6 tablespoons olive oil

2 medium onions, peeled and chopped

1 bay leaf

Sprig of fresh thyme

150 ml (¹/₄ pint) port

300 ml (¹/₂ pint) red wine

600 ml (1 pint) game, beef or chicken stock

4 teaspoons cornflour slackened to a paste with a little water

1 tablespoon redcurrant jelly

450 g (1 lb) puff pastry

1 egg, beaten

Method

Cut the game into bite-sized pieces and toss in the seasoned flour until well coated. Shake off excess flour. Heat the oil in a large heavy-based saucepan and fry the meat in batches unto sealed and lightly browned. Return all the sautéed meat to the pan. Add the chopped onion, bay leaf and thyme, pour in the port, wine and stock then simmer for approximately 2 hours until the meat is tender.

Stand a pie funnel in the centre of a deep pie dish and when the game has cooked, strain off the liquid into a bowl and put the meat into the dish. Pour the cooking liquid into a saucepan and whisk in the slackened cornflour. Add the redcurrant jelly and simmer and stir until thickened. Pour a third of the liquid over the meat in the dish and reserve the remainder for serving.

Pre-heat the oven to 220ºC/425ºF/gas mark 7. Roll out the pastry slightly larger than the pie dish; lay a strip round the edge of the pie dish, brush with beaten egg and lay the pastry lid over the top. Pinch the edges together to seal and make a small incision on top of the pie funnel to let out the steam. Brush the top of the pie with the rest of the beaten egg, put in the oven and bake for 25–30 minutes until risen and golden brown.

Hedgerow Pheasant Casserole

The night was clear and bright with a full moon – a poacher's night. Ghostly figures flitted from tree to tree, a countryman on tip-toe carrying a wooden pole with a noose at the end, quietly loops it over a roosting pheasant. A sharp tug brings the bird down to the ground where it is quickly killed and hidden under the poacher's jacket.

(The Newbury Weekly News, Nikki Rowan-Kedge)

Ingredients to serve 6

1 brace of pheasant, plucked, drawn, and ready for the oven
100 ml (3¹/₂ fl oz) vegetable oil
3 rounded tablespoons plain flour seasoned with salt and pepper
85 g (3 oz) rindless, smoked streaky bacon, chopped
1 onion, peeled and chopped
1 level tablespoon plain flour for thickening
900 ml (1¹/₂ pints) chicken or vegetable stock
100 ml (3¹/₂ fl oz) sloe gin
4 sticks celery, washed and chopped
4 eating apples, peeled, cored and chopped
Grated rind and juice of 1 small lemon
10 juniper berries, crushed
1 level teaspoon coriander seeds, crushed
Sprig of rosemary, leaves chopped
1 bay leaf
3 teaspoons made mustard
2 level tablespoons redcurrant jelly
Sea salt and black pepper to taste

Method

Pre-heat the oven to 190ºC/375ºF/gas mark 5. If necessary, wash the pheasants under cold running water, dry with kitchen paper. Trim away loose pieces of skin, feathers and lumps of yellow fat.

Heat the oil in a large oven-and-stove-proof casserole. Roll the pheasants in the seasoned flour and sauté in the hot oil until golden brown. When well browned, remove the pheasant and set aside. Put the bacon and onion into the pan and sauté until the bacon fat begins to run and the onion is soft. Sprinkle in the tablespoon flour and cook for 2 minutes, then pour in the stock and sloe gin, mix well and add all the rest of the ingredients. Season to taste and bring to simmering point.

Return the pheasants to the casserole, cover with the lid and cook in the pre-heated oven for 2¹/₂–3 hours depending on the age of pheasant, until the meat is tender . Test by inserting the point of a knife into the leg of the pheasant. Then lift the pheasant from the casserole onto a board. Skim off any fat that may be floating on top of the juices in the pan. Joint the pheasants, remove loose bones and return the pheasant potions to the casserole. Keep warm until required.

Cook's note
The sauce can be liquidised for a smoother texture before returning the jointed pheasant to the casserole if desired.

Sautéed Pheasant Breasts with Chestnut Sauce

If you've not had much luck on the moors, missed every bird, got soaked in the butts, and your Labrador just wouldn't come back when called, this dish will make you feel better and you may even agree with Oscar Wilde's quote in the late 1800s 'After a good meal, you can forgive anyone, even your own family.'

Ingredients to serve 4

1 tablespoon vegetable oil

55 g (2 oz) unsalted butter

6 shallots, peeled and chopped

4 pheasant breasts (from young birds)

1 large clove garlic, crushed

1 small glass medium white wine

450 ml (³/₄ pint) game or chicken stock

30 peeled and cooked fresh or frozen
   chestnuts – reserve a few for garnish

1 teaspoon tarragon, chopped

2 teaspoons parsley, chopped

Sea salt and black pepper to taste

4 tablespoons double cream

2 teaspoons redcurrant jelly

Method

Put the oil and butter into a large heavy-based pan and when the butter has melted put in the chopped shallots and cook until just turning brown. With a slotted spoon, remove the shallots from the pan and put in the pheasant breasts. Sauté on both sides until brown. Add the crushed garlic, wine, cooked shallots, stock and the prepared chestnuts. Simmer for 15–20 minutes until the pheasant is tender, timing depending upon thickness of the pheasant breasts.

When cooked, remove the pheasant from the pan and keep warm on a dish under kitchen foil. Boil the juices in the pan quickly until reduced by approximately a quarter and then transfer to a food processor. Blend until smooth and creamy. Add the cream, redcurrant jelly, chopped tarragon and parsley to the food processor and blend again for a few seconds. If the sauce is too thick, add a little water and whiz again.

Slice the pheasant breasts and arrange on a warm serving dish, pour over the sauce and serve dotted with the reserved chestnuts and, if you have time, crisply fried bacon rolls.

Venison and Beer Hot-Pot

There was a door into an old chapel; which had been long disused for devotion; but in the pulpit, as the safest place, was always to be found a cold chine of beef, a venison pasty, a gammon of bacon, or a great apple-pye with thick crust, well baked. He (the reverend Hastings) lived to be a hundred; never lost his eyesight, nor used spectacles. He got on horseback without help; and rode to the death of a stag till he was past fourscore.

(Mr Hastings, William Gilpin)

Ingredients to serve 4

450 g (1 lb) venison steak, cut into pieces

Sea salt and freshly ground black pepper to taste

2 tablespoons olive oil

2 large onions, peeled and chopped

60 g (2¼ oz) plain flour

300 ml (½ pint) chicken or game stock

300 ml (½ pint) real, dark ale

1 tablespoon clear honey

Method

Season the venison with the salt and pepper. Heat the oil in a large frying pan and sauté the venison for a few minutes to seal in the juices and until just turning brown. Remove from the pan and put into a large saucepan. Put the chopped onion into the frying pan and cook until just beginning to soften and turn brown, then remove and put with the venison. Put the flour into the frying pan and cook until beginning to brown. Pour in a little of the stock and simmer until thickened slightly, then put with the venison. Pour the remaining stock over the venison, add the beer and honey, check the seasonings, stir to mix, then cover the pan and cook gently for approximately 2–2½ hours until the venison is tender.

Wild Duck with Apricots

The duck come in on whispering wings. Mallard and teal rise with a rush, swing round in high airy circles, plane down again on bent wings.

(Wild Wings and Some Footsteps, J. Wentworth Day)

A mallard will serve two and a teal will be enough for one.

Ingredients to serve 4

2 mallard or 4 teal, plucked, cleaned and
  oven ready
2 or 4 sprigs fresh thyme
Sea salt and freshly ground black pepper
600 ml (1 pint) apple juice
55 g (2 oz) softened butter

For the sauce

200 g (7 oz) fresh apricots, stoned
1 liqueur glass Cointreau
150 ml ($^1/_4$ pint) double cream or light crème
  fraîche

Method

Pre-heat the oven to 220ºC/425ºF/gas mark 7. Place the duck in a roasting tin and push a sprig of fresh thyme into the cavity of each duck. Rub a little sea salt over the duck and grind over black pepper. Pour half the apple juice into the tin, smear the butter over each of the birds. Roast in the pre-heated oven for 20–30 minutes for teal, depending on pinkness of the meat and 1 hour for mallard.

Roasting time for mallard is 20 minutes to each 450 g (pound) and 20 minutes extra for larger birds.

To make the sauce Cook the apricots in the remaining apple juice until soft. Transfer to a food processor, pour in the Cointreau and blend until smooth. Return to a saucepan. Remove the cooked birds from the roasting tin, add a little water to the pan juices, scrape round and pour into the sauce. Stir in the cream or crème fraîche and heat gently. Serve separately.

PUDDINGS

Blackberry and Hazelnut Roulade

It was frequently past two [in the afternoon] before the breakfast party broke up. Then for the amusement of the morning, there was reading, fencing, single-stick, or shuttle-cock, in the great room; practising with pistols in the hall; walking-riding-cricket-sailing on the lake…between seven and eight we dined; and our evening lasted from one, two or three in the morning..

(Charles Skinner Matthews staying at Newstead Abbey, home of Lord Byron, 1809)

Crème de Mûres is a rich blackberry liqueur, well worth hunting for in wine merchants. If it is not available, a miniature of Cassis will be fine as will Grand Marnier if you prefer.

Ingredients to serve 6–8

For the roulade

7 eggs, separated

170 g (6 oz) caster sugar

100 g (3½ oz) roasted hazelnuts, finely ground

100 g (3½ oz) ground almonds

2 teaspoons baking powder

A little sifted icing sugar for turning out

For the filling

300 ml (10 fl oz) double cream

Icing sugar to taste

4 tablespoons Crème de Mûres

450 g (1 lb) blackberries, washed

Method

To make the roulade

Pre-heat the oven to 180ºC/350ºF/gas mark 4. Line a Swiss roll tin about 30 x 20 cm (12 x 8 inches) with oiled baking parchment oil side down to keep it in place. Allow at least 5 cm (2 inches) of parchment beyond the edges of the tray. Grease the paper with a little butter.

Beat the egg yolks and sugar together in a mixing bowl until thick and creamy. In a separate bowl mix together the ground hazelnuts, almonds and baking powder and then fold into the egg and sugar mixture. In another bowl, whisk the egg whites until stiff then fold into the egg and nut mixture. Pour into the prepared tin, shaking the mixture into place. Do not spread with a knife as this destroys the air bubbles and will make the roulade a little heavy. Bake in the pre-heated oven for 20–25 minutes until firm to the touch.

When cooked, remove the roulade from the oven and allow to cool. Take a new sheet of baking parchment and sprinkle with sifted icing sugar. Have the tin as close to the parchment as possible, and turn it upside down onto this new baking parchment. The roulade should come away from the tin onto the paper. Peel away the lining parchment.

To make the filling Whip the cream and sweeten to taste with the icing sugar. Blend in the blackberry liqueur (to taste) and blend it well with the cream mixture until it just holds its shape. Spread the blackberry cream onto the roulade and sprinkle two-thirds of the blackberries evenly over the cream. Roll up the roulade from the longest edge. (If you find this a daunting prospect, cut the roulade in half lengthways and sandwich together as you would for a gateau.) Decorate the top of the roulade with the remaining blackberries.

Cook's note
For decoration, swirls of cream can be dotted on top of the roulade along with the blackberries. You can also try alternative liqueurs and autumn fruits.

Black Treacle Mousse

Sir, you are in snug quarters here. A sensible, discreet person, your hostess, though a little gruff at first brush. Sir, all good cooks are so. They know their own value – they are a privileged class – they toil in a fiery element – they lie under a heavy responsibility.

(Institution of the Cleikem Club, *Cook and Housewife's Manual*, Mistress Margaret Dods)

Ingredients to serve 6

170 g (6 oz) caster sugar

6 large eggs, separated

3 tablespoons black treacle

3 sheets leaf gelatine, soaked in a little cold water

75 ml (2¹/₂ fl oz) boiling water for gelatine

225 ml (8 fl oz) whipping cream

Method

Put the sugar and egg yolks into a heat-proof glass bowl, stand it over a pan of simmering water, whisk together the sugar and egg yolks until thick and creamy. Add the black treacle and remove from the heat. Dissolve the sheets of gelatine in the boiling water, allow to cool a little and then fold into the mousse mixture. Whisk the cream and fold into the mousse. Whisk the egg whites until just holding shape and fold into the mousse. Blend well and pour into serving dish or individual glasses. Refrigerate to chill and set.

Bread and Butter Pudding

(From His Royal Highness The Prince of Wales)

An ancient pudding with many variations. The secret of its success lies in letting the pudding stand for an hour prior to baking – this allows the bread to swell and absorb the liquid, which gives a light, crusty pudding.

The addition of brandy turns this traditional nursery pudding into a pudding of sophistication. After trying this recipe, we saw why it is so favoured by the Prince.

Ingredients to serve 4–6

Crustless slices of buttered quality bread, enough to line a 1 litre (1³/₄ pint) ovenproof dish.

4 tablespoons each of raisins and sultanas

2 bananas, peeled and sliced

3 eggs

600 ml (1 pint) whole milk

Soft brown sugar or Demerara to taste

2–4 tablespoons brandy depending on preference

Cinnamon for sprinkling

Method

Cut the buttered slices of bread into triangles. Butter the ovenproof dish and arrange the bread in layers, sprinkling each layer with the fruit and finishing with a layer of bread, butter side up. Push any raisins and sultanas beneath the surface to prevent burning. Beat the eggs, milk and brandy together. Sprinkle the sugar and cinnamon over the pudding. Pour in the blended egg, milk and brandy. Allow to stand for approximately one hour before baking.

Pre-heat the oven to 180ºC/350ºF/gas mark 4. Bake for 30–40 minutes until the pudding is well risen with a golden crusty top. Serve immediately.

Cook's note
If home-made bread is not possible use a good quality organic loaf, perhaps one made by the Duchy of Cornwall bakery.

Country Treacle and Ginger Tart

Gone the sunset-wild and ruddy,
The West roars a song;
And a windy twilight's falling
And it's lonesome as can be.
Ere you hear the wild geese calling
Off the cold wet sea.

(Patrick Chalmers in *Wild Wings and
Some Footsteps*, J. Wentworth Day.)

Ingredients to serve 4

170 g (6 oz) shortcrust pastry
2-3 lumps preserved ginger, cut into small pieces
6 tablespoons golden syrup
55 g (2 oz) fine white breadcrumbs
Juice and grated rind of 1 small lemon

Method

Pre-heat the oven to 190°C/375°F/gas mark 5. Stand a 15-cm (6-inch) round flan ring on a baking tray. Roll out the pastry into a circle slightly larger than the flan ring and line the flan ring with the pastry so that the pastry comes up the sides of the ring.

Scatter the ginger pieces over the flan base and scatter over the breadcrumbs, spoon in the syrup, sprinkle over lemon rind, and juice. Put the tart in the pre-heated oven and cook for 25–30 minutes.

Cool slightly before serving as the hot syrup makes it too hot to eat.

Roasted Pears in Kirsch Syrup

A versatile pudding, which can be served hot or cold. Kirsch is optional. Almost any liqueur can be used – just choose your favourite.

Ingredients to serve 4

4 ripe pears, peeled, cut in half, core removed

3 tablespoons apple juice

3 walnut sized pieces of butter

1 tablespoon soft brown sugar

1 tablespoon clear honey

3-4 tablespoons Kirsch or other liqueur

4 fresh figs

Method

Pre-heat the oven to 180ºC/350ºF/gas mark 4. Stand the pears in an ovenproof dish and pour over the apple juice. Melt the butter and pour over the pears; add the sugar, honey and liqueur. Bake in the pre-heated oven until the pears are just softening, basting frequently with the syrupy juices in the pan. When the pears are soft, remove the dish from the oven and put the pears to one side.

Pear and Ginger Crumble

Ingredients to serve 4

For the crumble

170 g (6 oz) wholemeal flour

55 g (2 oz) plain flour

¹/₄ teaspoon salt

115 g (4 oz) butter or margarine

3 tablespoons Demerara sugar

55 g (2 oz) pecan nuts, roughly chopped

For the filling

900 g (2 lb) fresh pears, peeled, cored, cut into large chunks

4 whole pieces preserved stem ginger in syrup, thinly sliced

2 tablespoons soft brown sugar

Grated rind and juice of 1 small lemon

Method

Pre-heat the oven to 180ºC/350ºF/gas mark 4.

To make the crumble Sift both flours with the salt and put into a food processor including any bits of bran left in the sieve. Add in the butter or margarine cut into pieces and whiz until the mixture resembles fine breadcrumbs. Add the Demerara sugar and chopped pecan nuts. Whiz again briefly to mix.

To make the filling Lay the pieces of pear in a pie dish, cover with the slices of preserved ginger including a little of their syrup. Sprinkle over the soft brown sugar, lemon rind and juice. Sprinkle over the crumble mixture. Bake in the pre-heated oven for 35–40 minutes until the top is golden brown. If the top browns too quickly, cover loosely with kitchen foil.

CAKES

Melton Hunt Cake

Dickinson & Morris have been making this cake at Melton Mowbray in Leicestershire since 1854, supplying the members of the Melton Hunt, where it was customary to eat a slice of the cake with a glass of sherry or 'stirrup cup' while mounted on horseback waiting to begin the hunt. The original recipe has not changed since it was first made, but it does, however, remain a secret. Dickinson & Morris kindly sent us a 'version' of the cake, to which we have made a couple of additions, which we trust, will keep the flavour and wholesomeness of the original recipe.

Ingredients to serve 6–8

100 ml (3¹/₂ fl oz) dark Jamaica rum

350 g (12 oz) currants

140 g (5 oz) raisins

170 g (6 oz) butter, softened

170 g (6 oz) soft brown sugar

3 large eggs

Grated rind of 1 lemon and 1 orange

225 g (8 oz) plain flour sifted with 1 teaspoon mixed spice

85 g (3 oz) blanched almonds, roughly chopped

115 g (4 oz) glacé cherries cut in half

For decoration

6 whole cherries

12 whole almonds

Method

Pre-heat the oven to 150ºC/300ºF/gas mark 2. Grease and line an 18-cm (7-inch) round cake tin with baking parchment. Heat the rum in a small saucepan, remove from the heat and then drop in the currants and raisins, and leave to cool and soak in the rum.

Beat the butter and sugar together until soft and creamy; beat in the eggs one at a time. Blend in the lemon and orange rind. In batches add the flour, blanched almonds, halved glacé cherries and the soaked fruit including the rum. Keep mixing until there are no 'pockets' of flour. Pour the mixture into the prepared cake tin, smooth the top, dot over with the whole cherries and almonds. Bake in the centre of the pre-heated oven for 3 hours; after 1³/₄ hours cover the top with kitchen foil to prevent over-browning. Cool in the tin and turn out when ready.

Honey and Pecan Nut Muffins

It is all very well for us to smile at croquet and the archery of ladies wearing crinolines, but we must not forget that these innovations paved the way for golf, lawn-tennis, and at least half the sports we now enjoy.

(The Pleasure of your Company, June and Doris Langley Moore, 1933)

These delicious muffins make a pleasant change for breakfast. Pull the cooked muffins apart when buttering them as cutting with a knife compress the dough and makes them soggy.

Ingredients to make 24 muffins

Butter for greasing tins

250 g (9 oz) plain flour

2 teaspoons baking powder

1 teaspoon cream of tartar

60 g (2¼ oz) caster sugar

½ teaspoon salt

2 small eggs, beaten

5 tablespoons butter, melted

4 tablespoons clear honey

70 g (2½ oz) sultanas

100 g (3½ oz) pecan nuts broken into small pieces

150 ml (¼ pint) whole milk

Method

Pre-heat the oven to 200ºC/400ºF/gas mark 6. Grease 2 muffin tins with the butter, or line with paper cases each of which holds 12.

In a large mixing bowl, sift together the flour, baking powder, cream of tartar, sugar and salt. Stir in the beaten egg, butter, honey and a quarter of the milk. Blend well together then pour in the remaining milk. Mix well again. Fill the tins two-thirds full with the mixture and bake in the pre-heated oven for 20–25 minutes until risen.

When ready, remove from the oven and allow to cool slightly before removing from the tins.

Fruit and Almond Cake

At small country race meetings and gymkhanas there is often a preference for hamper luncheon baskets eaten picnic-wise in the host and hostess's car.

(Entertaining away from home, *The Pleasure of Your Company*,
Doris and June Langley Moore)

Ingredients to serve 8–10

500 g (1 lb 2 oz) unsalted butter

450 g (1 lb) caster sugar or soft bown

Grated rind of 1 lemon

8 eggs, beaten

550 g (1¼ lb) plain flour

2 teaspoons mixed spice

1 teaspoon baking powder

500 g (1 lb 2 oz) raisins

125 g (4½ oz) crystallised lemon and orange
  peel chopped

60 g (2¼ oz) split, blanched almonds

Method

Pre-heat the oven to 180ºC/350ºF/gas mark 4. Grease a 20-cm (8-inch) round, loose-sided cake tin and line the bottom with a circle of greaseproof paper.

Into a food processor put the butter, sugar and grated lemon rind, blend until creamy then pour in the beaten egg and blend again for a couple of minutes. Add the flour, mixed spice and baking powder, and blend once more until smooth. Turn out into a mixing bowl and stir in the raisins and crystallised peel. Pile the cake mixture into the tin, level the top and push the blanched almonds into the top of cake in a circle. Bake in the pre-heated oven for 2½ hours until cooked through. For the last ½ hour of cooking, lower the temperature

If the cake begins to brown too quickly, lay a piece of kitchen foil over the top.

Malted Wholemeal Bread

Hungry hunters and shooters triumphant and bemired from the chase, love to quench their thirst and spoil their dinners under the stuffed heads in the great hall, and golfers and fishermen to magnify their exploits amid the miscellaneous companionship of the hotel lounge. All these confess the hour with grateful pleasure, but the true spiritual home of the tea-pot is surely in a soft-lighted room, between a deep arm chair and a sofa cushioned with Asiatic charm, two cups only, and these of thinnest china, awaiting their fragrant infusion, whilst the clock points nearer to six than five, and a wood fire flickers sympathetically on the hearth.

(*Kitchen Essays*, Tea Time, Lady Jekyll)

Ingredients to make 2 large or 3 small loaves

250 g (9 oz) strong white flour	2 teaspoons soft light brown sugar
450 g (1 lb) wholemeal flour	1 tablespoon malt
3 level teaspoons salt	450 ml (³/₄ pint) warm water
1 sachet fast action dried yeast	4 tablespoons light olive oil

Method

Mix both flours in a large bowl with the salt and dried yeast and make a well in the centre. Put the sugar and malt into the warm water, stir and pour into the well of flour. Pour in the oil and mix to a smooth elastic dough. Turn the dough out onto a board and knead for 5 minutes and then put the dough into a clean bowl, cover with a greased plastic bag and leave in a warm place to prove and rise for 2 hours.

After that time, pre-heat the oven to 220ºC/425ºF/gas mark 7. Turn out the dough and cut into 2 or 3 loaves, shape and put onto a greased baking tray(s). Cover and leave to prove again for 25 minutes until puffy. Bake in the pre-heated oven 40–45 minutes, depending on the size of the loaves.

DRINKS

The Bowhill and Drumlanrig Specials

The first requisite for a grouse-shooter is patience, the next, a determination to make himself comfortable under any circumstances – and to put up with any inconveniences.

(Thomas Oakleigh)

Recipes kindly supplied by The Duke of Buccleuch and Queensberry, K.T.

The Bowhill special
For each cup of Bovril add one measure of cheap port or sweet sherry and one measure of brandy. Heat as usual and transport in a vacuum flask.

The Drumlanrig special
Strongly recommended for cold shooting days, at almost any hour.
For each cup of Bovril a double measure of whisky. Heat and transport in a vacuum flask.

PRESERVES

Apple Marmalade

Ripe eating apples are necessary for this apple marmalade. The sugar is measured against the quantity of apple purée, so the apples will need to be cooked to a pulp before measuring quantities.

Apple marmalade can be added to stews and casseroles instead of the more usual red currant jelly as well as adding to mayonnaise (see page 145).

(see page 145)

Ingredients

Well-flavoured eating apples
450 g (1 lb) granulated sugar to each 600 ml (1 pint) apple purée

Method

Wipe the apples and cut into quarters, no need to peel or core. Put the apples into a large preserving or heavy-based saucepan with sufficient water to cover. Cook over a low heat, stirring frequently until reduced to a thick pulp. Push the pulp through a sieve into a bowl.

Rinse out the pan the apples were cooked in. Measure the apple pulp and to every 600 ml (1 pint) add 450 g (1 pound) granulated sugar. Put the pulp and sugar into the pan and cook, stirring continuously until it resembles jam; the mixture should be thick enough so that a wooden spoon drawn across the base of the pan leaves a channel which does not close again.

When ready, pot and seal in clean jars until required.

Crab Apple Jelly

Crab apples were used in medieval times for making a type of vinegar called verjuice, which was much in use until lemons and limes became popular. This apple jelly is the perfect accompaniment to cold meats, game, pâtés and potted meats.

Ingredients

1.8 kg (4 lb) crab apples, washed, stalks removed
Juice of 1 lemon
2.2 litres (4 pints) water
Granulated sugar – 450 g (1 lb) to each 600 ml (1 pint) apple liquid

Method

Put the apples into a large saucepan, add the lemon juice and water. Simmer until the apple is soft and then strain the liquid through a jelly bag or fine sieve into a bowl. Measure the apple liquid and to each 600 ml (1 pint) add 450 g (1 pound) sugar,

Put the apple juice and sugar into a pan and cook over a moderate heat, stirring all the time until the sugar has dissolved, then boil rapidly until the temperature registers 110ºC/220ºF on a sugar thermometer. This is setting point. Test by putting a little jelly onto a cold saucer – if it sets and 'wrinkles' it is ready. Remove from the heat and allow to cool before putting into jars.

Autumn Fall Chutney

I love the fitful gust that shakes
The casement all the day,
And from the mossy elm tree takes
The faded leaves away,
Twirling them by the window pane
With thousand others down the lane.

(*The Shepherd's Calendar*, John Clare)

Ingredients to make approximately 3–4 kg of chutney

900 g (2 lb) apples, peeled, cored and
  chopped
900 g (2 lb) stoned plums, chopped
450 g (1 lb) onions, peeled and chopped
115 g (4 oz) raisins
450 g (1 lb) green tomatoes

225 g (8 oz) marrow flesh, cut into cubes
2 teaspoons mixed spice
450 ml (³/₄ pint) malt vinegar
115 g (4 oz) soft dark brown sugar
1 level teaspoon sea salt

Method

Put all the ingredients into a large heavy-based pan or preserving pan. Bring to the boil and then simmer until the fruit is tender and pulpy, and the mixture has thickened and the vinegar reduced. Remove from the heat, and pot in the usual way.

Cook's note
A few chopped dates and prunes can be added if desired.

Marrow and Ginger Chutney

Mr Sponge having got two bountiful slices (of ham) with a knotch of home-made bread, and some mustard on his plate, now made for the table, and elbowed himself into a place…

(*Mr Sponge's Sporting Tour*, R.S. Surtees)

Our friend Mr Sponge would have also helped himself liberally to this chutney if it had been on Mr Springwheat's sideboard. It is an excellent accompaniment for ham and other cold meats or potted game.

Ingredients to make approximately 8–10 225 g (8 oz jars)

1.6 kg (3¹/₂ lb) marrow, peeled, seeded and chopped

1 level teaspoon sea salt

550 g (1 lb 4 oz) shallots, peeled and chopped

550 g (1 lb 4 oz) apples, peeled, cored and chopped

2 teaspoons green peppercorns

5-cm (2-inch) piece of fresh root ginger, peeled and finely chopped

500 g (1 lb 2 oz) sultanas

115 g (4 oz) Demerara sugar

750 ml (1¹/₄ pints) malt vinegar

Method

Put all the ingredients into a large heavy-based pan or preserving pan. Bring to the boil, reduce the heat and simmer until the mixture thickens with very little liquid left. Stir often. When ready, remove from the heat and bottle and seal in the usual way.

Cook's note
If you don't want your kitchen to smell of cooking, cook the chutney on a barbecue in the garden (if it isn't raining). No smell and no mess.

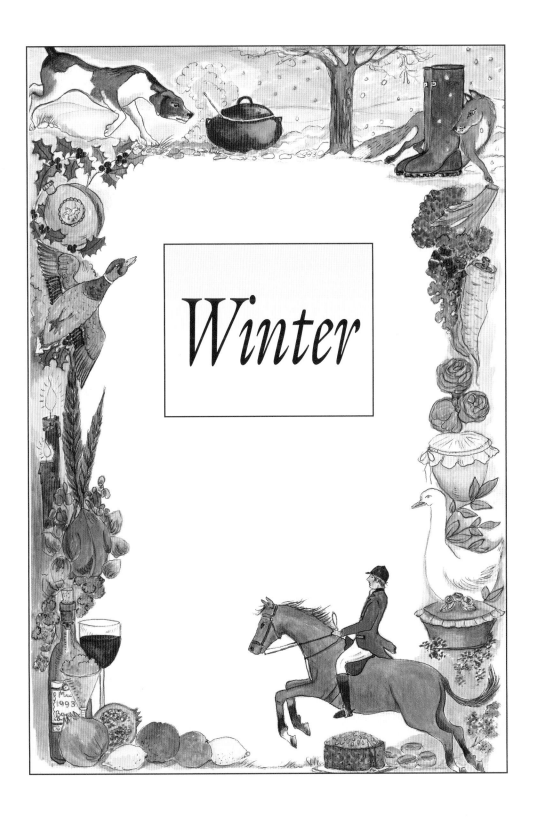

Winter

SOUPS

Butter Bean and Bacon Soup

This is a soup for emergencies or when battening down the hatches in stormy weather as it is made with store cupboard rations which can always be to hand.

Ingredients to serve 4

4 tablespoons olive oil

4 rashers rindless, smoked, streaky bacon, finely chopped

1 large onion, peeled and finely chopped

1 small clove garlic, crushed

425 g (15 oz) tin butter beans, drained

1 teaspoon coriander seeds, crushed

Sea salt and freshly ground black pepper to taste

750 ml (1¼ pints) chicken or vegetable stock

125 ml (4 fl oz) single cream

1 tablespoon parsley, freshly chopped

Method

Heat the oil in a saucepan and put in the bacon. Fry until brown and crispy then remove from the pan and put to one side. Put the onion into the saucepan and cook until soft; add the crushed garlic, butter beans and coriander seeds. Pour in the stock, season to taste and simmer for 20 minutes. Remove from the heat. Allow to cool slightly and liquidise until smooth. Return to the pan, add the bacon and cream and heat through gently. Serve sprinkled with chopped parsley.

Cook's note
If the electricity is off, it doesn't matter that the soup cannot be liquidised – it will just be more of a butter bean 'stew'.

Cream of Green Pea and Leek Soup

On a perishing November morning we found ourselves floundering in pitch darkness, across the salt marshes…

   We climbed in and out of muddy creeks half full of water until we arrived at the edge of the tide.

(*A Square Mile of Old England* – Game Birds and Wildfowl,
Aubrey Seymour)

Ingredients to serve 4

3 tablespoons olive oil
2 medium sized leeks, trimmed and chopped
2 small sticks celery, washed and chopped
1 clove garlic, crushed
1 litre (1³/₄ pints) vegetable or chicken stock
Sea salt and freshly ground black pepper to taste
280 g (10 oz) frozen peas
4 tablespoons double cream

Method

Heat the oil in a saucepan, add the leeks, celery and garlic, cook over a moderate heat until the vegetables begin to soften, stirring all the time. Pour in the stock, season to taste and simmer for 10 minutes. Then add the peas and simmer for a further 10 minutes. Remove from the heat and allow to cool slightly before liquidising until smooth. Return to the saucepan, add the cream and re-heat gently when ready to serve.

Roast Parsnip Soup

The cold sleet is drizzling down; the damp hangs upon the housetops and lamp-posts, and clings to you like an invisible cloak. The compound of ice, snow, and water on the pavement is a couple of inches thick.

(Early Coaches, from Sketches by Boz, *Charles Dickens)*

This warming soup would be much appreciated on such a day as the one described by Charles Dickens. It uses up any left-over roast parsnips or you can use freshly roasted ones if preferred. If time is short, bags of roasted parsnips can be found in the chiller counter of most supermarkets.

Ingredients to serve 4-6

85 g (3 oz) unsalted butter or 4 tablespoons olive oil

2 large onions, peeled and chopped

1 clove garlic, crushed

3 teaspoons curry paste

1 litre ($1^{3}/_{4}$ pints) chicken or vegetable stock

150 ml ($^{1}/_{4}$ pint) milk

6 small or 4 medium roast parsnips, chopped

Sea salt and freshly ground black pepper to taste

150 ml ($^{1}/_{4}$ pint) single cream

Method

Melt the butter or heat the oil in a saucepan and fry the onion until soft. Add the garlic, curry paste, stock, milk and chopped roast parsnip; season to taste, cover and simmer for 10 minutes. Remove from the heat and allow the soup to cool slightly before putting into a food processor. Liquidise until smooth and return the soup to the saucepan. Stir in the cream, check the seasonings and re-heat but do not boil.

Smoky Bacon and Lentil Soup

'The mornings are colder on the marshes. We woke yesterday in the decoy cottage to a dawn of thin and ghostly mist… The bulrushes stood stiff and brown, glittering with drops of moisture. It was all very still and ghostly. Yet, in the white unseen world about us there was a new and urgent stir. A stirring of wings and bird voices, which were not there a week ago.'

(Wild Wings and Some Footsteps, J. Wentworth Day)

Most of us at some time have experienced those chilly days of a bleak, cold winter. A cupful of this tasty and nourishing soup will warm up the 'inner man'. If transporting, use a wide-necked flask otherwise serve in soup bowls or cups.

Ingredients to serve 6–8

170 g (6 oz) smoked streaky bacon rind removed

2 onions, peeled and chopped

1 large leek, washed and chopped

2 large carrots, peeled and chopped

2 sticks celery, washed and chopped

250 g (9 oz) red lentils, soaked overnight in cold water

1 litre (1³/₄ pints) chicken or vegetable stock

1 bouquet garni

Cayenne pepper and sea salt to taste

Method

Cut the bacon into small pieces and fry in a pan until just turning brown (a little oil can be added if necessary). Remove the bacon and put to one side. Put in the onion and fry until just turning brown and then add the chopped vegetables and cook until slightly browned. Drain the lentils and put into a large saucepan, pour in the stock and add the fried vegetables, onion, bacon, bouquet garni, cayenne pepper and salt to taste. Bring to the boil and then simmer for 45 minutes.

When cooked, remove from the heat, discard the bay leaf and decant into a wide-necked flask or soup bowls.

STARTERS AND SIDE-DISHES

Duck and Brandy Terrine

Maria's performance was faultless; in half a minute she had laid a bird at my feet, a very large pale drake, quite unlike any other drake I had ever seen: Out of the silence that followed came a thin, shrill voice from over the hill: 'Thim's Mrs Brickley's ducks.'

(*Further Experiences of an Irish R.M.*, E. OE. Somerville and Martin Ross)

Ingredients to serve 6–8

225 g (8 oz) rindless streaky bacon

900 g (2 lb) duck meat, minced

450 g (1 lb) sausage meat

Freshly ground black pepper to taste

1–2 teaspoons sea salt

2 shallots, peeled and finely chopped

8 juniper berries, crushed

Grated rind of 1 large orange

2 teaspoons root ginger, freshly grated

2 cloves garlic, crushed

2 eggs, beaten

75 ml (2$^1/_2$ fl oz) brandy

Method

Pre-heat the oven to 200ºC/400ºF/gas mark 6. Line an ovenproof dish with the rashers of bacon. Into a large bowl put the minced duck and sausage meat, pepper, salt, chopped onion, crushed juniper berries, orange rind, garlic and grated ginger. Mix well together and then add the beaten egg and brandy. Mix thoroughly and put into the bacon-lined dish.

Cover with a double thickness of kitchen foil. Stand the ovenproof dish in a roasting dish half-filled with water. Cook in the centre of the pre-heated oven for 1$^3/_4$ hours, turning down the temperature after the first hour of cooking time to 190ºC/375ºF/gas mark 5. The terrine will shrink from the sides when it is cooked. Remove from the oven, allow to cool, then cover with greaseproof paper and refrigerate overnight. When required, turn out onto a board and slice.

Gunpowder Rarebit

Gunpowder Mustard is made by an old family firm. It is described as a fiery, explosive preparation guaranteed to wake up the taste buds. It is still sold today in the Houses of Parliament and is also available from good butchers and supermarkets. This recipe is a variation on the customary Welsh rarebit and to give it its traditional character, the slices of bread must come from unsliced farmhouse bread or, better still, a home-made loaf.

Ingredients to serve 4

4 tablespoons English butter

4 rashers rindless, smoked streaky bacon, cut into pieces

250 g (9 oz) strong Cheddar cheese, grated

2 level teaspoons Gunpowder Mustard

2 free-range egg yolks, beaten

$^1/_2$ level teaspoon paprika or cayenne pepper

50 ml (2 fl oz) dark ale

4 thick slices farmhouse bread

Method

Melt the butter in a frying pan and cook the bacon pieces, then tip the contents of the pan into a double saucepan. Beat in the grated cheese, mustard powder, beaten egg yolks and paprika or cayenne pepper. Stir in the ale and stand the double saucepan over a moderate heat. Cook until well blended and the cheese has completely melted.

Toast the bread, spread the Gunpowder rarebit mixture over the toast and put under the grill to brown.

Cook's note

English mustard powder will suffice if Gunpowder Mustard is not to your taste but it will not have the same flavour. Bacon rashers can be laid over the top of the cheese and grilled either as extra bacon or instead of putting the pieces into the mixture. The rarebit mixture can be kept in the refrigerator until required for a day or two and then spread on toast and grilled the same as above.

Parsnip and Celeriac Patties

Never serve parsnips straight from the water, any more than you would appear at the dinner table dripping from the bath. Only asparagus and Aphrodite can get away with it.

(*The Vegetable Book*, Jane Grigson)

These patties are suitable served with a green salad for vegetarians, or as a side-dish for shooting lunches.

Ingredients to serve 4

25 g (1 oz) unsalted butter
25 g (1 oz) plain flour
150 ml (¹/₄ pint) whole milk
Sea salt and freshly ground black pepper to taste
225 g (8 oz) parsnips, cooked and puréed
225 g (8 oz) celeriac, cooked and puréed
55 g (2 oz) toasted, finely chopped hazelnuts
1 egg, beaten
Wholemeal breadcrumbs for coating
Vegetable oil for deep-frying

Method

Melt the butter in a small saucepan and stir in the flour. Pour in the milk and bring to the boil, stirring all the time. Season well to taste. Put the parsnips, celeriac and chopped nuts into the milk and flour mixture, and blend well together. Turn the mixture onto a board and spread to form a 'cake'. Allow to cool, and make into small patties to your required size. Put the beaten egg into a dish and put the breadcrumbs into another dish. Dip the patties first into the beaten egg and then roll them in the breadcrumbs. Fry in hot oil until golden-brown.

Smoked Cheese 'Sausages'

English cookery was English cookery – when dining tables at English inns were well fortified for the (culinary) attack.

(Coaching Days and Coaching Ways, – The Inns on the Bath Road,
W. Outram Tristram)

For centuries, people sat inside the home or inn inglenook fireplace, drew the curtains and inhaled the smoke, believing it preserved the body and was a healthy thing to do. Even babies were wrapped in a blanket and placed up the chimney in the belief that the smoke prevented the little one from diseases – the belief was, if smoking preserved food, it must also preserve the human body!

Ingredients for 6–8 sausages

115 g (4 oz) brown breadcrumbs

100 g (3$^1/_2$ oz) grated smoked cheese
  (Applewood or any hard, smoked cheese)

2 shallots, peeled and finely chopped

$^1/_2$ teaspoon parsley, finely chopped

$^1/_2$ teaspoon tarragon, finely chopped

$^1/_2$ teaspoon cayenne pepper

1 level teaspoon dry mustard

Sea salt and freshly ground black pepper to
  taste

1 small egg, beaten

A little flour for coating

Vegetable or olive oil for frying

Method

Mix together all the ingredients except for the flour and beaten egg. Gradually blend in the beaten egg to bind the ingredients together. Cut the mixture into small portions and roll on a floured board into 'sausage' shapes. Dip the 'sausages' into the flour to cover then fry in the hot oil until nicely brown all over. Serve with smoked ham sauce (see page 221).

FISH

Anchovy Toast

A crimson smoulder in the West;
The last late crow had won to rest;
A breath of ice that gripped the chest –
And freezing died the day.

(*Melton and Homespun*, J. M. M. B. Durham
'Marshman' and R. J. Richardson)

Creamier than the commercial anchovy paste, this is a very simple dish to prepare – one that will be welcome for breakfast, tea-time, lunch, supper or as a savoury alternative to puddings for a dinner party. It keeps well in the refrigerator for 7–10 days.

Ingredients to serve 4–6

4 small tins anchovies, drained
4 tablespoons milk
4 tablespoons double cream

225 g (8 oz) unsalted butter
Freshly ground black pepper to taste

Method

Soak the drained anchovies in the milk for 4 minutes to remove most of the salt. Drain off the milk. Put the anchovies into a food processor and blend to a paste. Add the cream and blend again. Blend in the butter – a little at a time. Season with the pepper to taste and blend briefly. Transfer the anchovy paste to an earthenware pot and cover. Spread on hot toast when required.

Baked Pike with Onion and Herb Sauce

Izaak Walton in *The Complete Angler* (1653) portrays the pike as a freshwater wolf – probably because the pike devours all other fish that come within its territory. But first, catch your pike. If this is not possible, salmon or trout can be used instead. If you are fortunate enough to have caught or been given a pike, it needs soaking before cooking because of its coarse flesh. Cooking time is measured by the thickest part of the fish, 10 minutes per 2.5 cm (1 inch). If you have the time and feel inclined to do so, the skin can be taken off the pike before serving.

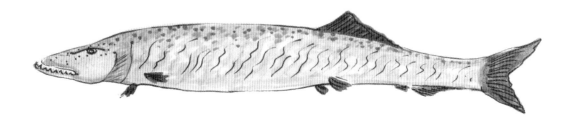

Ingredients to serve 3–4

1 pike approximately 450 g (1 lb) in weight after head and tail
  has been removed and the fish cleaned ready for cooking
Anchovy paste (see page 180)
Sea salt and freshly ground black pepper to taste

For the sauce

4 tablespoons olive oil
1 large onion, peeled and thinly sliced
Juice of 1 lemon
3 tablespoons light crème fraîche mixed with 3 tablespoons cold water
1 large sprig fresh basil, washed and chopped
Sea salt and freshly ground black pepper to taste

Method

For the fish
Pre-heat the oven to 220ºC/425ºF/gas mark 7. Wash the fish if necessary and lay on a sheet of kitchen foil. Dot 4–5 small knobs of anchovy paste inside the fish, season to taste and wrap the fish in the foil sealing the edges well. Bake in the pre-heated oven for 10 minutes to 2.5 cm (1 inch).

To make the sauce Heat the oil in a large frying pan, put in the onion and cook until just turning soft. Pour in the lemon juice, slackened crème fraîche and chopped basil leaves. Season to taste and cook for 3–4 minutes.

When the fish is cooked, remove from the oven, undo the foil and reserve the juices for pouring over the pike.

Fish Quenelles with Orange Sauce

Quenelles are small dumplings made from minced meat or fish, bound with egg whites and cream, poached and served in a cream sauce. They were once very popular and could be found regularly on restaurant menus and in dining rooms during the first half of the twentieth century. For a main dish large quenelles are made; for a first course, smaller ones; and tiny quenelles for garnishing soups and stews. The secret is to chill the ingredients well before using, this makes it easier to form the dumplings.

Ingredients to serve 4

2 egg whites

450 g (1 lb) skinless whiting fillets or any white fish fillets

125 ml (4 fl oz) double cream

Sea salt and freshly ground black pepper

For the sauce

Finely grated rind and juice of 1 small orange and 1 small lemon

125 ml (4 fl oz) double cream

3 large egg yolks

150 ml ($\frac{1}{4}$ pint) wine such as Chardonnay or white Côtes du Rhône

A little cayenne pepper to taste

Sea salt and freshly ground black pepper

60 g ($2\frac{1}{4}$ oz) unsalted butter

2 tablespoons clear honey (optional if a sweeter sauce is required)

1 tablespoon parsley, freshly chopped to serve

Method

Put the egg whites and the pieces of fish into a food processor and blend until smooth. Add the cream and season really well. Transfer to a bowl and chill in the refrigerator for at least an hour, longer if possible, before using.

To make the sauce Put the orange and lemon juice into a basin, stir in the cream, egg yolks and wine. The sauce may look as though it is curdling at this stage, don't worry; it all comes together as it cooks.

Set the basin over a saucepan of simmering water and whisk continuously until the mixture has the consistency of thin cream. Season to taste with the cayenne pepper, salt and black pepper and blend in the grated orange and lemon rind. Cut the butter into tiny pieces and beat piece by piece into the sauce. Keep the sauce hot but not boiling. Add the honey at this stage if using and allow to melt into the sauce. Set aside while you poach the quenelles.

Remove the chilled quenelle mixture from the refrigerator and form the mixture into egg shapes – use 2 tablespoons dipped in hot water and scoop the mixture from one spoon to another. Poach in lightly salted simmering water for 10–15 minutes. When all the quenelles are poached, drain well and place on a warm dish then spoon over the warm orange sauce. Sprinkle with chopped parsley to garnish, and serve.

Scottish Kipper Pâté with Whisky and Lime

This delicious pâté is an excellent starter for a dinner party and will happily wait, ready on the table, until all your guests have arrived.

Ingredients to serve 4

8 kipper fillets

2 tablespoons whisky

60 g (2¼ oz) butter

4 tablespoons natural yoghurt

Cayenne pepper to taste

Grated rind and juice of 1 lime

Sprigs of fresh parsley and slices of lime for
  garnish

Method

Poach the kipper fillets in a little water until just cooked; this should take around 3–4 minutes. Strain and remove any skin and bones. Liquidise the fillets with the whisky, butter, yoghurt, cayenne pepper, lime juice and rind. When the mixture is smooth, pour into individual serving pots or ramekins and allow to cool, then cover with cling film and refrigerate until required. When ready to serve, garnish with a small head of parsley and a twist of lime. Serve with warm oat cakes or hot toast.

Smoked Haddock with Poached Egg

The squire always breakfasted on hunting mornings at 4 a.m. The meal consisted of underdone beef washed down with eggs beaten up in brandy, and thus fortified, he was prepared for a fifty-mile ride if need be. It was no unusual thing to see Tom Moody, his famous whipper-in, taking the hounds to covert before daylight, and they would often stick to the sport till it was too dark to see the hounds.

('Squire' George Forester, told by Thormanby)

A deliciously simple breakfast dish should there be no beef or eggs in brandy on the sideboard. It is also good for lunch, high tea or supper.

8 rounded tablespoons Basmati rice

55 g (2 oz) butter

1 medium onion, peeled and chopped

550 g (1¼ lb) undyed smoked haddock fillets

100 ml (3½ fl oz) milk

2 teaspoons cornflour mixed with a little milk

150 ml (¼ pint) single cream

4 eggs

Sea salt and freshly ground black pepper to taste

1 tablespoon parsley, chopped

Method

Cook the rice in salted water until tender. Melt the butter in a frying pan, put in the onion and cook until soft. Add the fish and milk and poach the fish for 10–15 minutes depending on thickness of the fillets. When cooked, remove the haddock from the pan and put onto a warm serving dish.

Pour the slackened cornflour into the milk in the pan, cook and stir until the liquid begins to thicken, then stir in the cream. Turn the heat right down and drop in the eggs to poach in the milky sauce.

Divide the rice between 4 plates, place the haddock fillets on the bed of rice and place a poached egg on top of each fillet. Season to taste and sprinkle over chopped parsley to serve.

MAIN COURSES

Carbonade of Vegetables with Cheese Scone Topping

When we came within a town, and found the church clocks all stopped, the dial faces choked with snow, and the inn-signs blotted out, it seemed as if the whole place were overgrown with white moss. As to the coach, it was a mere snowball. One would have thought this enough: notwithstanding which, I pledge my word that it snowed and snowed, and it still snowed, and it never left off snowing.

(Stopped by the Snow, from *Christmas Stories*, Charles Dickens)

Those cold and hungry travellers would no doubt have appreciated a dish such as this comforting carbonade, rich in flavour – the absence of meat is not noticeable.

Ingredients to serve 4–6

4 Jerusalem artichokes, peeled and thinly sliced
1 red pepper, de-seeded and cut into small pieces
4 carrots, peeled and sliced
2 parsnips, peeled and chopped
1 leek, washed and chopped
2 cloves garlic, crushed
4 tablespoons vegetable oil
150 ml ($^1/_4$ pint) water
150 ml ($^1/_4$ pint) dry white wine
1 tablespoon yeast extract (Marmite or similar)
Sea salt and freshly ground black pepper to taste

For the scone topping

115 g (4 oz) wholemeal flour

115 g (4 oz) plain flour

Pinch of salt

2 teaspoons baking powder

85 g (3 oz) margarine

100 g (3$^1/_2$ oz) Cheddar cheese, grated

150 ml ($^1/_4$ pint) milk

Method

Put the chopped and sliced vegetables into a large saucepan, add the garlic and oil, and sauté for 2–3 minutes. Stir in the water, wine and yeast extract, season to taste, bring to the boil and then simmer for 20 minutes or until the vegetables are almost cooked and the liquid has thickened a little. Pour into a large casserole or earthenware ovenproof dish.

Pre-heat the oven to 200ºC/400ºF/gas mark 6.

To make the scones Sift the two flours, salt and baking powder together, rub in the margarine and grated cheese, reserving 3 tablespoons of cheese for sprinkling. Mix in sufficient milk to form a smooth dough, reserving 2 tablespoons for glazing. Roll out the dough approximately 1 cm ($^1/_2$ inch) thick and cut out circles, about 5 cm (2 inches) in diameter (a standard wine glass should be just about right). Lay the scones around the edge of the casserole, leaving the centre clear. Brush the scones with the reserved milk and sprinkle the remaining grated cheese over the top of the casserole. Put the casserole into the pre-heated oven and bake for 15 minutes to heat through.

Spicy Duck Sausages

Ingredients to serve 4

450 g (1 lb) duck breast, minced

4 rashers rindless, smoked, streaky bacon, finely chopped

250 g (9 oz) sausage meat

70 g (2¹/₂ oz) white breadcrumbs

4 sage leaves, chopped

1 teaspoon ground ginger

¹/₂ teaspoon cayenne pepper

Sea salt and freshly ground black pepper to taste

A little plain flour for dusting

Olive oil for frying

Method

Put all the ingredients, except the flour, into a large mixing bowl and blend thoroughly together. Form into sausage shapes, dust with the flour and chill for an hour or so, or overnight, before frying. Serve with a spicy tomato sauce (see page 222).

Turkey Fillets with Lime and Green Grape Sauce

Excellent for last-minute dishes – fillets of turkey or chicken do not take long to cook. In fact, care must be taken, not to over cook them, else they become tough and 'rubbery'.

Ingredients to serve 4

55 g (2 oz) unsalted butter

2 small sticks celery, white part only, finely chopped

4 shallots, peeled and finely chopped

150 ml (¹/₄ pint) chicken stock

Juice and grated rind of 1 lime

4 tablespoons light olive oil

450 g (1 lb) turkey fillets

1 level tablespoon cornflour mixed with 75 ml (3 fl oz) water

115 g (4 oz) seedless green grapes

100 ml (3¹/₂ fl oz) double cream

Sea salt and freshly ground black pepper

Method

To make the sauce Melt the butter in a saucepan, put in the celery and onion, and cook until soft. Pour in the stock, simmer for 10 minutes and then add the grated rind and lime-juice. Remove from the heat and set aside.

Heat the olive oil in a frying pan put in the turkey fillets in batches and sauté on both sides until nicely brown. Remove from the pan and keep warm. Deglaze the frying pan with 2 tablespoons of the sauce scraping all the meat juices and pour into the rest of the sauce in the saucepan.

Return the sauce to the heat and add the slackened cornflour. Simmer and stir until the sauce has thickened. Add the grapes and stir in the cream, season to taste and re-heat gently to warm through. Pour the sauce over the turkey fillets and serve.

Goose Roasted with Prune, Quince and Apple

There never was such a goose. Bob said he didn't believe there ever was such a goose cooked. Its tenderness and flavour, size and cheapness, were the themes of universal admiration. Eked out by apple sauce, mashed potatoes, it was a sufficient dinner for the whole family.

(A Christmas Carol, Charles Dickens)

Ingredients to serve 6-8

1 oven-ready goose weighing approximately 5 kg (10-11 lb)

Sea salt and freshly ground black pepper to taste

450 g (1 lb) apple flesh, after removing peel and core

225 g (8 oz) quince flesh, after removing peel and core

225 g (8 oz) stoned prunes, chopped

4 sage leaves, finely chopped

2 level tablespoons soft brown sugar

300 ml (½ pint) chicken or vegetables stock

300 ml (½ pint) medium-sweet cider

4 teaspoons redcurrant or crab apple jelly

Method

Pre-heat the oven to 190ºC/375ºF/gas mark 5. Wipe the inside of the goose with kitchen paper and place on a wire rack inside a large roasting tin. Prick the skin all over with a fork to allow the fat to run. Rub the goose all over with salt and sprinkle black pepper over. Put the apple, quince, prunes, sage leaves and sugar in a mixing bowl and mix well together. Push inside the cavity. Roast in the pre-heated oven for $3^1/_2$–4 hours. Test by inserting a fork into the thickest part of the leg – if the juices run clear, your goose is cooked. When ready, remove from the oven and place on a warm serving dish. Remove the wire rack from the roasting tin and skim off the fat, keeping it for roasting potatoes. Pour the meat juices into a saucepan. Pour the stock and cider into the gravy and boil rapidly for approximately 15 minutes until reduced slightly. Beat the redcurrant or crab apple jelly into the gravy. If a thicker gravy is required, stir in a tablespoon of cornflour mixed with 4 tablespoons of water. Whisk well into the gravy.

Hashed Pheasant

After dinner we opened a hamper of game sent by the Venables, and found in it a pheasant, a hare, a brace of rabbits, a brace of woodcock and a turkey.

(*Kilvert's Diaries*, Monday 26th December 1870)

An excellent way to use up left-over game; the flavour comes from the quality of the gravy and claret.

Ingredients to serve 4

55 g (2 oz) unsalted butter

1 medium onion, peeled and chopped

1 clove garlic, crushed

225 g (8 oz) cold, cooked pheasant meat, cut into small pieces

600 ml (1 pint) game or beef stock

100 ml (3½ fl oz) good quality claret

Sea salt and freshly ground black pepper

2 teaspoons redcurrant jelly

1 tablespoon dark orange marmalade

Method

Melt the butter in a saucepan and put in the onion. Cook until soft and then add the garlic and pheasant pieces. Move the meat quickly around the pan to brown slightly and then pour in the stock and claret. Season to taste, simmer for 15 minutes and then stir in the redcurrant jelly and marmalade. Cook for a further 5 minutes stirring often, check the seasonings and serve.

Pork and Bean Hot-Pot

An easy-to-prepare dish for picnics, easily transportable in a food vacuum flask. It can be heated on the barbecue or on the stove and served in bowls – great for a party dish in the country style. Made the day before, it leaves you free to entertain on the day itself with the minimum of work still to do.

Ingredients to serve 6–8

3–4 tablespoons light olive oil or butter, whichever you prefer

500 g (1 lb 2 oz) lean shoulder of pork, any skin and most of the fat removed

4 rashers rindless, smoked, streaky bacon cut into pieces

500 g (1 lb 2 oz) packet dried haricot beans (soaked overnight in cold water)

2 cloves garlic, peeled and crushed

1 x 400 g (14 oz) tin chopped tomatoes

2 teaspoons brown sugar

2 teaspoons Dijon mustard

1 tablespoon fresh thyme, chopped

Sea salt and ground black pepper to taste

550 ml (19 fl oz) chicken or vegetable stock

Method

Pre-heat the oven to 170ºC/325ºF/gas mark 3. Heat the butter or oil in a frying pan, put in the pieces of pork and fry until lightly brown, then remove from the pan. Sauté the bacon pieces and put with the pork. Grease a deep ovenproof earthenware casserole and put the pork and bacon into the pot. Drain the water from the soaked beans and mix the beans into the pork and bacon. Stir in the crushed garlic, tomatoes, sugar, mustard and chopped thyme. Season to taste and pour in the stock. Secure the lid or cover tightly with kitchen foil and cook in the pre-heated oven for 3–3$^{1}/_{2}$ hours. Serve with peppered, creamed potatoes or warm crusty bread.

Pot-Port Braised Pheasant

'At the dinner table the Rector glowed with austere geniality while he carved a brace of pheasant which represented a day's covert shooting he'd had with Lord Dumborough.'

(*Memoirs of a Fox-Hunting Man,* Siegfried Sassoon)

Ingredients to serve 4

6 tablespoons olive oil

4 rashers, rindless, smoked streaky bacon

4 oven-ready pheasant breasts

1 stick celery, washed and chopped

1 small onion, peeled and thinly sliced

1 medium carrot, peeled and cut into 'matchsticks'

1 bay leaf

100 ml (3^1/$_2$ fl oz) beef or chicken stock

50 ml (2 fl oz) tawny port

Sea salt and freshly ground black pepper

Method

Pre-heat the oven to 180ºC/350ºF/gas mark 4. Put one tablespoon of the oil into a large heavy-based frying pan and fry the bacon until just softening. Remove the bacon and put into an ovenproof casserole dish. Put a little more oil into the pan and brown the pheasant breasts on both sides. Remove from the pan and put to one side – not in the dish. Pour the remaining oil into the pan and put in the celery, onion and carrot; and sauté until slightly coloured. Tip the vegetables along with the oil into the casserole with the bacon. Put in the bay leaf and then lay the pheasant breasts, skin side uppermost on top of the vegetables. Pour in the stock and port, season to taste and cover, securing the lid tightly. A little kitchen foil may be needed to seal completely. Cook in the pre-heated oven for approximately 35–40 minutes until the meat is tender. Serve with peppered, creamed celeriac and buttered cabbage.

Cook's note
Cooking time may vary according to size and thickness of the pheasant breasts.

Roast Partridge in a Pear Sauce

Out of the dawn had a light snow drifted,
The line of the road was limned in white,
And over the edge of the world it lifted
Beautiful, burnished, broad and bright.

(The Golden Hoofprints from *Galloping Shoes,*
Will H. Ogilvie)

An excellent dish for a shooting lunch or celebration dinner party, visually appealing and appetising.

Ingredients to serve 4

4 partridge, plucked, cleaned and oven ready

2 cloves garlic, crushed

8 rashers smoked streaky bacon

150 ml ($^1/_4$ pint) dry vermouth

Sea salt and freshly ground black pepper to taste

5 just ripe pears

2 teaspoons clear honey

4 tablespoons single cream

2–3 small bunches watercress for decoration

Method

Pre-heat the oven to 220ºC/425ºF/gas mark 7. Rub each partridge with a little crushed garlic. Wrap each bird with two rashers of bacon and roast for 10 minutes and then reduce the temperature to 200ºC/400ºF/gas mark 6 and cook for 20–30 minutes depending on size of birds. Remove from the oven when ready, put on a serving dish, cover with kitchen foil and keep them warm while you make the sauce.

To make the sauce De-glaze the roasting pan by adding the vermouth to the meat juices, stir round and pour the juices into a saucepan. Season to taste. Peel and core 4 of the pears, cut into pieces and put with the meat juices. Cook for 2–3 minutes, remove from the heat and allow to cool slightly. Then put into a food processor, add the honey and cream, and blend quickly until smooth. Return the sauce to the saucepan and re-heat but do not boil. Peel, core and slice the remaining pear and arrange the slices around the partridge. Lay the bunches of watercress around the birds.

Serving suggestion Fried breadcrumbs, game chips and broccoli.

Roast Woodcock

'That frosty evening was followed by three others like unto it, and a flight of woodcock came in. I calculated that I could do with five guns, and I dispatched invitations to shoot to four of the local sportsmen, among whom was, of course, my landlord.'

(*Some Experiences of an Irish R. M.,* E. OE. Somerville and Martin Ross, 1899)

Ingredients to serve 2

2 oven-ready woodcock (1 per person)
1 small loaf white bread
Walnut-sized knob of butter, melted
4 rashers streaky bacon (2 rashers for each bird)
4 tablespoons brown breadcrumbs
Salt and black pepper to taste

Method

Pre-heat the oven to 200ºC/400ºF/gas mark 6. Cut two fairly thick slices of white bread, remove the crusts and place a bird on each slice. Brush each bird with melted butter and lay the bacon over the breasts. Season well to taste and put into a roasting tin. Roast in the pre-heated oven for 15 minutes.

When ready to serve, fry the breadcrumbs in a little oil or melted butter and serve with the roast woodcock accompanied, if wished, by bread sauce, sautéed potatoes and green beans.

Cook's note
If time is short, you can cheat on the potatoes and warm up a packet of good quality crisps, and serve as game chips instead.

Saddle of Hare with Blackberry Sauce

I mean 'are-unting'; it is a werry nice lady-like amusement; and though we have no 'are soup at dinner, I make no doubt we have some werry keen 'are-unters' at table for all that. I beg to give you 'are-unting', and the merry Dotfield 'Arriers.'

(Handley Cross, R. S. Surtees)

This recipe needs to be made a couple of days in advance, as the hare needs to be well marinaded – the finished product will be well worth the time taken.

Ingredients to serve 4

1 saddle of hare
2 tablespoons beef dripping or olive oil

For the marinade

1 clove garlic, crushed
600 ml (1 pint) cider
5 tablespoons raspberry vinegar
Large sprig of parsley and thyme
1 bay leaf
1 small onion, peeled and chopped

For the sauce

100 ml ($3^{1}/_{2}$ fl oz) brandy
450 g (1 lb) blackberries
4 teaspoons blackberry or redcurrant jelly
125 ml (4 fl oz) single cream

Method

Rub the garlic over the saddle of hare. Put the marinade ingredients into a large bowl and immerse the hare in the liquid. Marinade for at least 2 days in a cool place.

After that time remove the hare from the marinade and pat dry with kitchen paper then place in a roasting tin. Strain the marinade through a sieve and reserve the strained liquid for basting. Discard the contents of the sieve. *Pre-heat the oven to 230ºC/450ºF/gas mark 8.*

Rub the hare with the dripping or brush over with oil and roast in the pre-heated oven for 50 minutes until the meat is tender; baste often with the marinade. When cooked, remove the hare from the oven, place onto a dish and keep warm.

To make the sauce Remove any fat from the roasting pan and pour the juices and the remaining marinade into a saucepan. Add the brandy, blackberries, blackberry or redcurrant jelly and boil rapidly to reduce the liquid a little. Remove from the heat and stir in the cream. Pour the sauce into a sauceboat and serve with the roast hare decorated if wished with a few blackberries and sprigs of parsley.

Venison and Beef Steak Suet Crust Pudding

Made a day in advance this is a superb way of using venison. Perfect for a shooting lunch or hearty supper after a day in the country. When we serve this dish, the usual comment is that it is the best suet pudding they've ever eaten. Your patience in preparing it will be well rewarded.

Ingredients to serve 4–6

60 g (2¼ oz) beef dripping
2 medium onions, peeled and chopped
1 clove garlic, crushed with a little salt
1 bay leaf
350 g (12 oz) stewing venison, cut into cubes
350 g (12 oz) lean stewing beef, cut into cubes
900 ml (1½ pints) beef stock
Salt and freshly ground black pepper to taste
6 tablespoons port

For the suet pastry

Butter for greasing the dish
250 g (9 oz) self-raising flour
¼ teaspoon salt
¼ teaspoon freshly ground white pepper
1 teaspoon fresh tarragon, finely chopped
115 g (4 oz) vegetable suet
125 ml (4 fl oz) milk

Method

A day or two before the dish is to be served melt the dripping in a large saucepan, put in the onion and cook until soft. Add the garlic, bay leaf, venison and beef, and stir for a few minutes before pouring in the stock. Season well, cover and bring to the boil, then turn down the heat and simmer gently for 3 hours until the meat is tender. Strain the meat juices into a basin and keep the gravy and the cooked meat separately until required.

When required grease a 900-ml (1½-pint) basin with butter. Cut out a circle of greaseproof paper to fit the bottom and place it in the basin.

To make the suet pastry Put the flour, salt, pepper, tarragon and suet into a large mixing bowl and mix all ingredients well. Pour in the milk and stir to form a dough. If the mixture is too dry add a little more milk or water – the dough should be firm enough to roll out without sticking.

Separate one-third of the pastry to form a lid and set aside. Roll out the remaining pastry into a circle. Cut a 'V' shape out of the circle (this makes it easier to fit the basin) and line the basin with the suet pastry dough, pressing the edges firmly together to prevent seepage. Fill the lined basin with the meat. Roll the reserved suet pastry into a circle the size of the basin to form a lid. Place on top, pressing the edges of dough together. Cover the top with kitchen foil, scrunching up the edges to secure firmly around the edge of the basin. Do not make the top too tight or it will prevent the pudding from rising.

Steam the pudding for 1½ hours. When the pudding is almost ready, about 5–10 minutes from the end of cooking time, pour the gravy into a saucepan, add the port, heat through and pour into a warm sauceboat. Turn out the steamed pudding, or wrap a napkin around the basin and serve with the hot gravy.

Cook's note
If you prefer a lighter result, substitute olive or sunflower oil instead of beef dripping.

PUDDINGS

Brandied Orange-Filled Prunes

An unusual accompaniment for venison, duck, pheasant and chicken, as well as being a pudding in its own right.

Ingredients

36 large, stoned prunes (the bigger, the better)
Orange juice for soaking prunes
2–3 tablespoons Cognac, Armagnac or brandy
Grated rind and juice of 1 large orange

Method

Soak the prunes overnight in sufficient orange juice to cover.

Drain the prunes and remove stones if you haven't been able to buy stoned prunes. Put 20 prunes to one side. Put the remaining 16 prunes into a food processor, add the brandy, grated orange rind and juice. Blend until smooth. Spoon a little of the mixture into each of the reserved prunes, filling the cavity that held the stone.

Dark Chocolate Pudding with Whisky and Honey Sauce

Always the snow crunches underfoot. The winds bite your nose. The mist creeps clammily up your sleeves and down your collar. The whisky flask invites voluptuously – suddenly, the mist lifts – and on the opposite shoulder of the hill, you see a ghostly fresco of the tall deer moving against the sky.

(Wild Wings and Some Footsteps, J. Wentworth Day)

What a welcome this rich, inviting pudding will give to hungry hunters, home from the hills – perfect pudding for shooting lunches. Your guests will go off with a warm, satisfying glow that is certain to keep out the frosty weather.

Ingredients to serve 4–6

For the pudding
115 g (4 oz) caster sugar
115 g (4 oz) butter or margarine
2 eggs, beaten
1 teaspoon vanilla essence
25 g (1 oz) cocoa powder
55 g (2 oz) chocolate drops
170 g (6 oz) self-raising flour, sifted
2–3 tablespoons milk to mix

For the sauce
300 ml (¹/₂ pint) milk
1 rounded tablespoon cornflour, slackened with a little cold water
100 ml (3¹/₂ fl oz) whisky
Juice of 1 lemon
4 tablespoons clear honey
150 ml (¹/₄ pint) double cream

Method

To make the pudding Half fill a saucepan or steamer with water and put it on to boil. Grease a 900-ml (1^1/$_2$-pint) pudding basin. Cream together the sugar and butter or margarine until fluffy and pale. Mix in the beaten egg and vanilla essence and blend well together. Add a tablespoon of hot water to the cocoa powder and mix to a smooth paste, then blend into the pudding mixture. Blend in the chocolate drops and with a metal spoon, fold in the sifted flour, then add sufficient milk to give a 'dropping' consistency. Pour the mixture into the greased basin, cover with greaseproof paper or kitchen foil, secure with string, place it in the saucepan of boiling water and steam for 1^1/$_2$ hours. You may need to add a little more boiling water from time to time.

To make the sauce Heat the milk. Mix together the slackened cornflour, honey, whisky and lemon juice. Pour into the hot milk and stir for 2 minutes to cook the cornflour and thicken the sauce. Stir in the cream and keep warm until required.

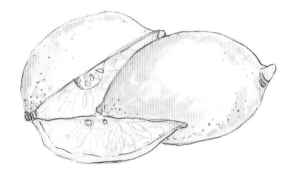

Hot Coffee Fudge Pudding

'It's putrid weather,' agreed Lady Lomondham, pouring herself another cup from the Georgian coffee-pot. 'Still, I think I'd better make a one-horse day of it.'
(Mustard Pot, Huntsman, Gilbert Frankau, from *The Horse Lover's Anthology*)

A delicious pudding for dinner or tea time; it separates during cooking, which produces its own sauce, it can be served with chilled sour cream or whipped cream flavoured with coffee essence if appetites and taste buds are up to it.

Ingredients to serve 6–8

170 g (6 oz) butter

200 g (7 oz) soft brown sugar

2 eggs, beaten

6 tablespoons coffee essence

250 g (9 oz) self-raising flour sifted with 1^1/$_2$ teaspoons baking powder

60 g (2^1/$_4$ oz) chopped walnuts

450 ml (15 fl oz) milk

Method

Pre-heat the oven to 170ºC/325ºF/gas mark 3. Beat the butter and 115 g (4 oz) of the sugar together until pale and fluffy. Gradually beat in the egg and the coffee essence. Fold in the sifted flour and chopped walnuts, adding a little milk to give a 'dropping' consistency. Spoon the mixture into a 1-litre (2-pint) buttered ovenproof dish. Mix together the remaining sugar and milk and pour over the pudding. Bake for 1 hour 25 minutes until spongy to the touch. Serve warm from the oven.

Hot Rum Bananas

The Exeter Fly has taken nearly three hours to come the seven miles from Hounslow. The landlord of The Bush, Staines, hearing this, follows the lead of the landlord of The George, and counsels rest and dinner; and the passengers, who to speak truly, have never before in their lives come so near to the experience of riding in the air in a hollowed-out iceberg, incline their ears to the advice.

(Coaching Days and Coaching Ways, W. Outram Tristram)

After an experience such as that, what a wonderful sight the inn lights must have been to the passengers and the valiant coachman. This pudding would certainly have warmed the hearts as well as the stomachs of these intrepid travellers. A deliciously satisfying pudding for any visitor returning home on a cold and snowy evening.

Ingredients to serve 4

85 g (3 oz) unsalted butter
4 large or 8 small firm, ripe bananas
6 teaspoons caster sugar
100 ml (3¹/₂ fl oz) dark rum
Juice of 1 lemon

Method

Melt the butter in a frying pan. Peel the bananas, cut in half and put them into the pan. Shake over the sugar, stir and cook until the butter and sugar start to caramelise, and turn the bananas over so they cook evenly.

When the butter and sugar has caramelised, pour in the rum and lemon juice. Remove the bananas and put onto a warm dish. Boil the liquid in the pan rapidly for 1 minute then pour over the bananas.

Serve with Greek yoghurt, single, double or clotted cream depending on preference.

Iced Cointreau and Raisin Mousse

Decorated with segments of fresh orange, and if close to Christmas, a small holly leaf, will impart a festive tone to this light and refreshing pudding.

Ingredients to serve 4

60 g (2¼ oz) seedless raisins

Juice and finely grated rind of 1 medium orange

1 small egg, separated

60 g (2¼ oz) caster sugar

3–4 tablespoons Cointreau

4 tablespoons natural Greek yoghurt

150 ml (¼ pint) double cream

Method

Put the raisins, orange juice and rind into a saucepan and place over a moderate heat until the liquid begins to simmer. Remove from the heat and put to one side to allow the raisins to soak up the liquid. Put the egg yolk, sugar and Cointreau into a bowl and whisk together until well blended. With a slotted spoon, remove the raisins from the orange liquid and put to one side. Whisk the orange juice into the egg and sugar mixture and return to the saucepan. Whisk the mixture over a low heat to cook the egg, and when ready, pour the mousse mixture into a bowl.

Whisk the yoghurt into the mousse and fold in the raisins. In a separate bowl whip the cream until it just begins to thicken then fold into the mousse.

In a clean bowl, whisk the egg white until it just holds its shape and fold into the mousse. Pour into ramekins or individual moulds and cover with cling film and freeze overnight. Remove from the freezer approximately 10 minutes before required and, when ready to serve, run a small knife around the inside edge of the ramekin or mould to loosen and turn out onto serving plates.

Pink Champagne, Pomegranate and Pink Grapefruit Sorbet

It was Michéle's husband's shooting weekend and her turn to entertain the shooting party and their wives that evening 'We drank nothing but champagne…'

(*The Frenchwoman's Kitchen*, Brigitte Tilleray)

A refreshing sorbet to round off any party, and very good for using up any leftover champagne from a previous celebration – if there is any left of course otherwise you'll just have to buy another bottle. Pour a little champagne over the finished sorbet just before serving and serve with rosé or white champagne if you prefer.

Ingredients to serve 4–6

150 ml (¹⁄₄ pint) pink champagne
350 g (12 oz) caster sugar
Juice of 2 pink grapefruit
Juice of 1 lemon
5 pomegranates

Method

Put the champagne and sugar into a saucepan and over a low heat. Dissolve the sugar and then bring to the boil to reduce a little and until it is a syrupy consistency – this will happen quite quickly. Remove from the heat, add the grapefruit and lemon juice. Halve the pomegranates and squeeze the juice through a sieve into the champagne sugar syrup and blend well together. Pour into a suitable container and freeze until required. Alternatively, the mixture can be put into an ice-cream maker and blended until frozen – this method gives a lighter, fluffier texture.

When required, remove from the freezer and use a spoon to scrape the sorbet from the container into a light 'snow' and pile into glasses or onto a pretty plate. Decorate with fresh raspberries or strawberries.

Cook's note
If using leftover champagne, it doesn't matter if it's flat.

Plum, Date and Cinnamon Crumble

A warming, festive alternative to Christmas pudding, retaining the customary ingredients but is a lighter option after the richness of a celebration dinner.

Ingredients to serve 4

450 g (1 lb) stoned plums

100 ml (3½ fl oz) water

225 g (8 oz) stoned dates, chopped

50 ml (2 fl oz) dark rum

85 g (3 oz) sultanas or raisins

85 g (3 oz) plain flour

85 g (3 oz) wholemeal flour

1 teaspoon cinnamon

100 g (3½–4 oz) unsalted butter or margarine

170 g (6 oz) Demerara sugar

Method

Pre-heat the oven to 200ºC/400ºF/gas mark 6. Put the plums into a saucepan with the water and cook until the plums are soft. Stir in the chopped dates, raisins and rum and transfer to an ovenproof dish.

Mix the two flours and the cinnamon together, then rub in the butter or margarine until the mixture resembles fine breadcrumbs. Mix in the sugar and sprinkle the crumble mixture over the fruit in the dish. Bake in the pre-heated oven for 30–40 minutes. Serve with cream or custard laced with a tablespoon of brandy or dark rum.

Rum and Raisin Semi-Freddo

' …We heard the strains of the quadrille band on the ice at Draycot. When it grew dark the ice was lighted with Chinese lanterns, and the intense glare of blue, green and crimson lights and magnesium riband made the whole place as light as day. Then people skated with torches.'

(*Kilvert's Diaries,* Wednesday 28th December 1870)

Ingredients to serve 4

4 tablespoons dark rum

85 g (3 oz) seedless raisins

3 eggs, separated

115 g (4 oz) caster sugar

Juice and grated rind of 1 small lemon

300 ml (¹/₂ pint) double cream

Method

Heat the rum in a saucepan, drop in the raisins, remove from the heat and set aside to allow the raisins to soak up the rum and swell. Over a pan of water, whisk the egg yolks, sugar, lemon rind and juice until thick and creamy. Remove from the heat and set aside. In a clean bowl, lightly beat the cream until it just holds its shape, check the rum and raisins are completely cold and fold them into the beaten cream. Mix this rum cream into the egg and sugar mixture. Whip the egg whites until stiff and fold into the cream and sugar mixture. Blend well in. Pour into individual ramekins, cover and freeze.

CAKES

Courgette and Sultana Muffins

There had been a sharp frost for some time, and no hunting to be had, and sporting undergraduates were at their wits' end what to do – some, indeed did scruple to say that if the weather did not change they should take to reading!

(*Sporting Days and Sporting Ways,* Ralph Nevill)

They could have taken tea and enjoyed these unusual muffins, it might have pacified them, for while, at least.

Ingredients to make 6–8 muffins

115 g (4 oz) self-raising flour

115 g (4 oz) wholemeal flour

$^1/_2$ teaspoon baking powder

Pinch of salt

$^1/_2$ teaspoon allspice

1 large egg

180 g (6 oz) soft brown sugar

100 ml (3$^1/_2$ fl oz) vegetable oil

1 large or 2 small courgettes, peeled and finely grated

90 g (3$^1/_4$ oz) sultanas

A little milk to mix

Method

Pre-heat the oven to 175ºC/350ºF/gas mark 4. Sift the two flours, baking powder, salt and allspice together into a mixing bowl. In a separate bowl beat the egg and sugar until light and creamy; add the oil and continue beating for 2–3 minutes and then stir in the grated courgette and sultanas. Fold this mixture into the sifted flour and allspice, blending in the ingredients adding a little milk to mix, but take care not to over mix, or the muffins will become heavy.

Spoon the mixture into a greased tartlet or muffin tin and bake in the pre-heated oven for 25–30 minutes until light brown in colour. Cool on a wire rack before serving with honey, whipped cream or butter.

Cook's note
Pull the muffins apart, they go soggy if cut with a knife.

Dark Treacle Gingerbread Cake

This is really a 'cake come pudding' wonderfully rich and 'sticky'. It can be eaten hot from the oven served with cream, or allowed to cool and served for tea as a traditional country cake.

Ingredients for 6–8 large slices

Softened butter for greasing
115 g (4 oz) dark soft brown sugar
115 g (4 oz) butter
150 g (5$^1/_2$ oz) black treacle
150 g (5$^1/_2$ oz) golden syrup
2 eggs, beaten
115 g (4 oz) plain flour
115 g (4 oz) wholemeal flour
3 teaspoons ground ginger
5 pieces preserved stem ginger pieces, chopped
60 g (2$^1/_4$ oz) sultanas
$^1/_2$ teaspoon bicarbonate of soda
4 tablespoons warm whole milk

Method

Pre-heat the oven to 160ºC/325ºF/gas mark 3. Grease a deep 20-cm (8-inch) loaf tin with the softened butter and line the bottom with a length of buttered greaseproof paper.

Cream the sugar and butter together, then stir in the treacle, syrup and beaten eggs. Sift the two flours and ground ginger together and mix into the sugar and treacle mixture. Stir in the preserved ginger pieces and sultanas. Stir the bicarbonate of soda into the warm milk and add to the cake mixture, blending all ingredients well together. Put the mixture into the prepared tin and bake in the pre-heated oven for 1$^1/_4$ hours. For a less 'sticky' cake cook for a further 10–15 minutes depending on preference.

Gamekeeper's Fruit Cake

Gamekeeper of Little Bedwyn Estate in Wiltshire, Michael Martin and his wife Gwen were married for 66 years. On the day of their wedding Gwen had to be carried into the church by the taxi driver because it was snowing so heavily. Every Christmas Gwen made this rich fruit cake. It can be iced or left plain. Wrap up a couple of slices and put them in your pocket to keep hunger pangs at bay when out in the country.

Ingredients to serve 10–12 depending on size of slices

650 g (1 lb 7 oz) butter
550 g (1 lb 4 oz) soft brown sugar
8 eggs, beaten
550 g (1 lb 4 oz) currants
550 g (1 lb 4 oz) sultanas
280 g (10 oz) raisins
350 g (12 oz) crystallised unbleached cherries
225 g (8 oz) crystallised lemon and orange peel, chopped
115 g (4 oz) ground almonds
Grated rind and juice of 1 lemon
$^1/_2$ teaspoon salt
2 level teaspoons ground mixed spice
650 g (1 lb 7 oz) self-raising flour
100 ml (3$^1/_2$ fl oz) brandy

Method

Pre-heat the oven to 150ºC/300ºF/gas mark 2. Line a 28-cm (11-inch) square cake tin with buttered greaseproof paper

In a large bowl, cream the butter and sugar together, beat in the eggs, add a little flour if the mixture separates, this will bind it together.

In a separate large bowl put all the other ingredients except for the flour and brandy. Mix well together. Put a third of the fruit mixture with the creamed butter and egg mixture, add a third of the flour and blend well together. Repeat this process until all ingredients are in one bowl and thoroughly blended with no pockets of flour.

Put the mixture into the cake tin, level it with a palette knife and scoop a shallow dip in the centre. Tie a double layer of brown paper around the edge of the cake tin and secure with string. Put a tray of boiling water in the bottom of the oven, this keeps the cake moist. Bake the cake in the centre of the oven for 6 hours. Check after 5 hours by inserting a skewer into the centre of the cake – if it comes out clean, it is ready.

Maple Butter Cake

And behold, on the first floor, at the court-end of the house, in a room with all the window curtains drawn, a fire piled halfway up the chimney, plates warming before it, wax candles gleaming everywhere, and a table spread for three…

(A Famous Inn from *Martin Chuzzlewit*, Charles Dickens)

This delicious cake can be served cold in the usual way or straight from the oven, drizzled with maple syrup, and served with pouring cream.

Ingredients to serve 4–6

115 g (4 oz) caster sugar

100 g (3$^1/_2$ oz) butter

3–4 tablespoons maple syrup

1 egg, beaten

2 tablespoons light crème fraîche

170 g (6 oz) self-raising wholemeal flour

$^1/_2$ teaspoon bicarbonate of soda

8 pecan nuts for decoration

Method

Pre-heat the oven to 180ºC/350ºF/gas mark 4. Line a small loaf tin 16 cm x 10 cm (6$^1/_2$ x 4 in) with greased greaseproof paper. Put the sugar and butter into a food processor and blend until smooth, add the maple syrup and beaten egg, and blend again and then blend in the crème fraîche. Sift the flour and bicarbonate of soda together and put into the food processor, and blend briefly to mix in the flour. Take care not to over mix or the cake will become too heavy. Turn the mixture out into the prepared loaf tin. Dot with the pecan nuts and bake in the pre-heated oven for 35–40 minutes.

When cooked through, drizzle one or two tablespoons of maple syrup over the top of the cake.

Pocket Ginger Flapjacks

These tasty little flapjacks are ideal for putting in your pocket to take with you for an energy giving snack when out hunting, shooting or fishing; children also love them at tea time or an emergency picnic nibble.

Ingredients to make approximately 12–14 flapjacks

170 g (6 oz) butter

140 g (5 oz) Demerara sugar

4 level tablespoons golden syrup

4 rounded teaspoons ground ginger

300 g (10¹/₂ oz) rolled oats

Method

Pre-heat the oven to 180ºC/350ºF/gas mark 4. Melt the butter in a medium saucepan; add the sugar and syrup blending well together. Remove from the heat and stir in the oats. Press the mixture evenly into a lightly greased, shallow, baking tray 18 x 30 cm (7 x 12 in) across. Put into the oven and bake for 25 minutes. The flapjacks should be light golden brown in colour. If your oven runs very hot, reduce the temperature by a few degrees to prevent the sugar from burning.

When ready, remove from the oven, cool slightly and then mark out the mixture into pocket-sized squares. Allow to cool completely in the baking tray before removing with a palette knife. Keep in an airtight container until wanted.

Cook's note
When measuring the syrup, use a heated metal spoon – the syrup slides off the spoon more easily.

SAUCES, STOCK AND MARINADE

Smoked Ham Sauce

A quickly made sauce to accompany smoked cheese 'sausages', also goes well with jacket potatoes, gammon steaks and roast chicken or turkey.

Ingredients for 4–6 servings

55 g (2 oz) unsalted butter
1 clove garlic, crushed
$^{1}/_{2}$ medium onion, peeled and very finely chopped
190 ml (6$^{1}/_{2}$ fl oz) milk
Freshly ground black pepper to taste
2 teaspoons cornflour, slackened with a little whole milk
6 tablespoons double cream
115 g (4 oz) thinly sliced and chopped smoked ham, cut into strips
2 teaspoons chives, freshly chopped

Method

Melt the butter in a saucepan, add the garlic and onion and cook for 2–3 minutes. Pour in the milk and season with the pepper. Add the slackened cornflour and stir to thicken, cook for 2 minutes and then stir in the cream. Blend in the strips of ham and chives, mix well together and serve.

Spicy Tomato Sauce

Serves as an accompanying sauce or as a dip for buffet parties.
A good standby as it freezes well

Ingredients to serve 4–6

4 tablespoons olive oil

1 medium onion, peeled and chopped

1 clove garlic, crushed

450 g (1 lb) ripe tomatoes, skinned and chopped

1 tablespoon tomato paste

150 ml (¹/₄ pint) vegetables or chicken stock

1 tablespoon parsley, chopped

2 level teaspoons sugar

1 teaspoon oregano

1 teaspoon ground white pepper

¹/₄ teaspoon cayenne pepper

Sea salt and freshly ground black pepper to taste

Method

Heat the oil in a saucepan, add the onion and garlic, and cook until the onion is just turning brown. Stir in the chopped tomatoes and then add all the remaining ingredients. Blend well together. Simmer for 45 minutes. The sauce can be liquidised if you prefer a smoother texture. Re-heat when required.

Quick Game Bird Stock

In the past, making stock was time consuming but here is a recipe for a quick and easy way of making good tasty stock.

Ingredients to make 500 ml (1³/₄ pints) of stock

Large knob of beef dripping

1 large Spanish onion

1 large carrot

2 bay leaves

1 cooked pheasant or other game bird,
  (if small birds use 2 carcasses)

1 tin condensed consommé

2 consommé tins of water

Method

Put the dripping into a large saucepan. Roughly chop the onion into chunks leaving the skin on and put into the pan. Peel and chop the carrot and add to the pan. Put in the bay leaves and bird carcass. Pour in the consommé and 2 tins of water, cover and bring to the boil. Reduce the heat to its lowest setting and simmer until the meat falls from the bone.

   Strain the stock into a bowl, allow to cool and put in the refrigerator until required. When the stock has set, the fat can be removed from the surface if not required.

For game bird soup Pour 1 tablespoon olive oil into a saucepan; slice 6 button mushrooms and chop 4 spring onions. Put into the pan and sauté in the oil until soft. Pour in the prepared stock, add the meat pieces, and season to taste with salt and black pepper. If desired a small glass of port can be added and thickened with a little cornflour, otherwise serve as a game consommé. Bring to the boil and serve immediately.

Cook's note
The remaining ingredients can be discarded but you can, if you have time, remove the meat from the carcass and put it into the stock and use for making a game soup. However, this must be cooked and eaten on the same day if using the meat.

Marinade for Venison

1 tablespoon vegetable oil

1 onion, peeled and chopped

3 shallots, peeled and halved

1 carrot, chopped

2 cloves garlic, chopped

Salt and pepper

1 bottle red wine

1 teaspoon crushed coriander seeds

2 sprigs fresh thyme

8 juniper berries, crushed

2 tablespoons redcurrant jelly

Method

Heat the oil in a large saucepan; add the vegetables, sprinkle in the seasonings and cook for 8 minutes. Pour in the wine and bring to the boil; lower the heat and add the crushed coriander seeds, thyme sprigs, crushed juniper berries and redcurrant jelly and simmer for 15 minutes. Allow to cool completely before pouring over the venison. Cover, and leave overnight in a cool place.

When ready, remove the venison, strain the marinade into a bowl and reserve the liquid for further use.

The marinade cannot be stored and used after it has had the meat marinating in it.

WEIGHTS AND MEASUREMENTS

Weights

		125 g	4$^1/_2$ oz	600 g	1 lb 5 oz
		140 g	5 oz	650 g	1 lb 7 oz
		150 g	5$^1/_2$ oz	700 g	1 lb 9 oz
10 g	$^1/_4$ oz	170 g	6 oz	750 g	1 lb 10 oz
15 g	$^1/_2$ oz	200 g	7 oz	800 g	1 lb 12 oz
20 g	$^3/_4$ oz	225 g	8 oz	850 g	1 lb 14 oz
25 g	1 oz	250 g	9 oz	900 g	2 lbs
35 g	1$^1/_4$ oz	275 g	9$^1/_2$ oz	950 g	2 lb 2 oz
40 g	1$^1/_2$ oz	280 g	10 oz	1 kg	2 lb 4 oz
50 g	1$^3/_4$ oz	300 g	10$^1/_2$ oz	1.25 kg	2 lb 12 oz
55 g	2 oz	325 g	11$^1/_2$ oz	1.3 kg	3 lbs
60 g	2$^1/_4$ oz	350 g	12 oz	1.5 kg	3 lb 5 oz
70 g	2$^1/_2$ oz	375 g	13 oz	1.6 kg	3 lb 8 oz
75 g	2$^3/_4$ oz	400 g	14 oz	1.8 kg	4 lbs
85 g	3 oz	425 g	15 oz	2 kg	4 lb 8 oz
90 g	3$^1/_4$ oz	450 g	1 lb	2.5 kg	5 lb 8 oz
100 g	3$^1/_2$ oz	500 g	1 lb 2 oz	2.7 kg	6 lbs
115 g	4 oz	550 g	1 lb 4 oz	3 kg	6 lb 8 oz

Oven Temperature

Centigrade	Fahrenheit	Gas	Centigrade	Fahrenheit	Gas
140°	275°	1	200°	400°	6
150°	300°	2	220°	425°	7
170°	325°	3	230°	450°	8
180°	350°	4	240°	475°	9
190°	375°	5			